To those who believe the
world can be put to rights
with a simple bowl of soup

NEW COVENT GARDEN FOOD Co

Soup for All Seasons

OUR FAVOURITE SEASONAL RECIPES

B⊞XTREE

New Covent Garden Food Company would like to thank everyone who so
generously gave us their recipes, and were happy to share them with all who
read our third recipe book. Too many to list in this space, they are mentioned
on the recipes themselves. We would, however, like to give special
thanks to our chief taster, Sian Gist and our text wizard, Chas Walton.

First published 2006 by Boxtree
an imprint of Pan Macmillan Ltd
Pan Macmillan, 20 New Wharf Road, London N1 9RR
Basingstoke and Oxford
Associated companies throughout the world
www.panmacmillan.com
ISBN-13: 978-0-7522-2619-4
ISBN-10: 0-7522-2619-3
Copyright © New Covent Garden Food Company 2006

A CIP catalogue record for this book is available from the British Library.
Colour Reproduction by Aylesbury Studios Ltd Bromley Kent.
Printed and bound in Great Britain by Butler and Tanner.

Contents

Introduction — 9

Larder Ingredients — 11

Simple Stocks — 12

Our Philosophy — 18

Autumn Recipes — 19

Winter Recipes — 45

Spring Recipes — 71

Summer Recipes — 97

Index — 123

Introduction

Soup is easy, down-to-earth, one-pot cooking. It's friendly, too. The aroma draws people into the kitchen as casually as it calls them to the table. They come because soup is different every time: bubbling with winter comfort, ripe with summer growth, mellow with autumnal plenty, bursting with the vibrancy of spring.

Soup brings us together at New Covent Garden Food Company. We share a delight in the endless variety of this simple, unfussy dish. Each day we try out something new, yet we're never short of tasters. They're a critical bunch, our colleagues, but good-natured, too – warmly appreciative when we get it right and joyfully rude when we don't.

But that's what experimentation is for. Between our chopping and their slurping, we work our way through the soup-chef's year. There's no mistaking the seasons here: we see them in the ever-changing bunches of ingredients that land on our chopping block.

Soup for All Seasons

We love working with the seasons. What kind of summer would it be if it wasn't marked by the pop of bright-green, sun-warmed pea pods? What winter can pass without mud, wellies and the scraping of soil from a newly dug parsnip? Fresh seasonal soup connects us to nature – to food at its best.

Soup for All Seasons is our introduction to the year-round harvest. Here you'll find tender yet rod-straight asparagus, crisp green sprouts snatched from the frost, crunchy celery with leaves that flutter in the late-summer breeze and juicy red beetroot within its jacket of midnight-maroon.

A year of recipes

Our year – the soup-maker's year – starts in autumn. That's when friends and families retreat to the kitchen, and root vegetables – the soup-cook's most dependable ingredient – come into season.

Autumn also marks the start of our recipe-testing cycle. Some we invent; some arrive by post or email from friends and strangers; some we adapt from foods we've seen on our travels; and some come from the army of cooks who rise to the annual challenge of our Student Chef and Create A Soup competitions.

This book contains recipes from all those sources. It represents the collective soup-fuelled wisdom of the wider New Covent Garden Food Company community – our chefs, our friends, our relatives, our suppliers, our supporters and our fellow cooks.

Don't be afraid

Soup making isn't difficult. It's as fun to play it by ear as it is to follow a recipe. Treat the recipes as a starting point rather than a destination. After you've reached for the saucepan, anything goes: a pinch of saffron, a richer stock, kale instead of cabbage, mutton instead of lamb, a dash of soy sauce, tomatoes left in the sun for an extra day or two, frozen peas instead of fresh. You never know till you try.

Soup is great for using what's to hand (leftovers, dried herbs, vegetables from the freezer) and making the most of passing bargains (bones from your butcher, market produce at closing time, the seasonal glut in a neighbour's garden). If you can cook it, you can probably make soup out of it.

Preparation times

The recipes include cooking times, but not preparation times. Preparation depends on the source of the ingredient and the cook. Washed and trimmed supermarket produce is ready in an instant; farmers' market veg takes longer. Some cooks like to scrub under a running tap; others prefer to peel.

Garnishes

We've not suggested garnishes unless the soup demands it. But that shouldn't stop you adding the occasional flourish. A few slivers of crispy bacon, a grating of fresh Parmesan or a leaf or two of watercress can make all the difference. Choose contrasting colours and textures to turn a simple soup into an event.

Healthy options

Fresh soup is intrinsically healthy. You can't go wrong with a bowlful of vegetable goodness. You can reduce the fat content of recipes that contain meat, cream or cheese – simply substitute low-fat dairy products, use crème fraîche instead of cream and trim excess fat from cuts of meat.

No time to cook?

No problem – simply pop down to your local store or supermarket and buy a carton (or two) from our delicious range of fresh soups. You'll find each one as good as the soups in this book.

Larder Ingredients

This book is about using what's in season. But even the most committed seasonal-soup chefs have a few year-round essentials in their larders. Here we've provided you with some useful core ingredients to keep in your larder for making soup. Put them on your shopping list now and you'll be ready when seasonal ingredients come your way.

Don't go overboard on the ingredient buying. It's easier – and far more economical – to use what you already have. You can make fabulous soup without ordering a vanload of goodies from your local delicatessen.

Oils	Extra Virgin Olive Oil Olive Oil Sunflower Oil	**Vinegars**	White-wine Vinegar Red-wine Vinegar Sherry Vinegar
Ready-to-Eat Fruits	Dried Apricots Dried Cranberries	**Sugar**	Dark Brown Muscovado Caster Sugar
Herbs & Spices	Sea Salt Peppercorns Bay Leaves Nutmeg Coriander Turmeric Garam Masala Ground Cumin Chilli Flakes Chilli Powder Smoked Paprika Vanilla Pods Saffron Strands Garlic	**Tomatoes**	Tinned Chopped Tomatoes Sun-dried Tomato Paste Passata
Beans & Pulses	Red Lentils Tinned Haricot Beans	**Mustard**	Dijon Wholegrain
Alcohol	Red Wine White Wine Champagne Port Dry Sherry Brandy Crème de Cassis Pale Ale	**Soy Sauce** **Worcestershire Sauce** **Basil Pesto**	

Simple Stocks

No matter how thick or chunky it looks, a soup is mostly liquid, so it pays to use the tastiest liquid you can lay your hands on. In short, it's worth making a jug of stock.

The good news is that stocks are easy to make. They're cheap, too – pretty close to getting something for nothing. If you can beg or borrow a few bones or offcuts from your butcher or fishmonger, you're halfway there. Stocks are also a great way of squeezing a last gasp of flavour from carcasses and leftovers. Don't bin anything until you've made stock from it.

The trick with stocks is to make them when you can, and to make far more than you need. Freeze what you can't use in bags packed in boxes (gives you a neat brick shape that stacks tidily in your freezer).

And, if you don't have any home-made stock to hand, use a stock cube. It may not be quite as good, but it will be quicker. And much better a quick home-cooked soup than no soup at all.

Here are our tried-and-tested stock-making tips:

- Give your stock time to develop – resist the temptation to stir, although you should skim off impurities from time to time.

- For a clear stock, bring to the boil from cold and simmer gently. Strain carefully, letting the moisture drip through the sieve – if you rub the contents through, your stock will turn cloudy. If necessary, strain a second time through muslin.

- Season lightly or, better still, not at all. You can always add salt and pepper to your finished soup, but you can't take it away.

- If you're buying bones from your butcher, ask him to chop them for you, otherwise, take your cooked bones and chop them into small pieces with a strong, large knife or meat cleaver on a thick chopping board.

Brown Beef Stock

Makes 8–10 pints   Cooking time: 8 hours

1 kg (2 lb 4 oz) beef bones, chopped into small pieces
500 g (1 lb 2 oz) veal bones (if you don't want to use veal bones,
simply substitute beef bones, adding the quantities together)
6 litres (10½ pints) water
2 tablespoons olive oil
3 small carrots, roughly chopped
1 medium onion, roughly chopped
1 large leek, roughly chopped
3 sticks celery, roughly chopped
150 g (5½ oz) tomatoes, roughly chopped
8 peppercorns, crushed
70 g (2½ oz) mushrooms, quartered

- Heat the oven to 200°C/gas mark 6.
- Remove any excess fat from the bones and place them into a roasting tin and cook in the oven for 50 minutes.
- Drain off any fat and transfer the bones to a large pan. Cover with water and bring to the boil, simmer for 20 minutes, skimming well to remove any excess fat.
- Heat the olive oil in a pan, add the carrots, onion, leek and celery. Cook for 10 minutes until browned, but not burnt; add to the bones and water pan.
- Add the tomatoes and peppercorns to the pan, bring to the boil and simmer for 6 hours, skimming frequently.
- Sieve the stock into a clean container and seal until required. Throw away the vegetables and bones.

Chicken Stock

Makes 8–10 pints

Cooking time: 8 hours

2 kg (4½ lb) chicken bones, chopped into small pieces

6 litres (10½ pints) water

3 small carrots, roughly chopped

1 medium onion, roughly chopped

1 large leek, roughly chopped

3 sticks celery, roughly chopped

8 peppercorns, crushed

- Place the bones into a large pan, cover with water, then bring to the boil and simmer for 20 minutes; skim off any excess fat.
- Add the vegetables and peppercorns, bring back to the boil and simmer for 8 hours, skimming frequently.
- Sieve the stock into a clean container and seal until required. Throw away the vegetables and bones.

Vegetable Stock

Makes 8 pints

Makes 8 pints

Cooking time: 3 hours

4 small carrots, roughly chopped

3 sticks celery, roughly chopped

2 medium leeks, roughly chopped

1 large onion, roughly chopped

6 litres (10½ pints) water

2 teaspoons peppercorns

1 bay leaf

2 cloves garlic, roughly chopped

- Place the vegetables into a large pan and cover with water, bring to the boil and simmer for 30 minutes, skim off any excess fat.
- Add the peppercorns, bay leaf and garlic cloves, then bring back to the boil and simmer for 2½ hours, skimming frequently.
- Sieve the stock into a clean container and seal until required. Throw away the vegetables.

Lamb Stock

Makes 8–10 pints   Cooking time: 8 hours

2½ kg (5½ lb) lamb bones, chopped into small pieces
6 litres (10½ pints) water
2 tablespoons olive oil
3 small carrots, roughly chopped
1 medium onion, roughly chopped
1 large leek, roughly chopped
3 sticks celery, roughly chopped
150 g (5½ oz) tomatoes, roughly chopped
8 peppercorns, crushed
70 g (2½ oz) mushrooms, quartered

- **Heat the oven to 200°C/gas mark 6.**
- **Place the bones into a roasting tin and cook in the oven for 50 minutes.**
- **Drain off the fat, transfer the bones to a large pan, then cover with water. Bring to the boil and simmer for 20 minutes; skim off any excess fat.**
- **Heat the olive oil in a pan, add the carrots, onion, leek and celery. Cook for 10 minutes until browned, but not burnt, then add to the bones and water pan.**
- **Add the tomatoes and peppercorns, bring to the boil and simmer for 6 hours, skimming frequently.**
- **Sieve the stock into a clean container and seal until required, throw away the vegetables and bones.**

Fish Stock

Makes 10–12 pints   Cooking time: 45 minutes

75 g (3 oz) butter

2 medium onions, roughly chopped

6 peppercorns, crushed

25 g (1 oz) parsley stalks, roughly chopped

1 lemon, juice of

2 kg (4½ lb) fish bones (sole, turbot or whiting), washed

5 litres (8¾ pints) water

1 bay leaf

- Melt the butter in a pan, add the onions, peppercorns, parsley stalks and lemon juice and cook for 15 minutes without colouring.
- Add the fish bones to the pan, cover and simmer for 5 minutes, avoid browning.
- Add the bay leaf and water, bring to the boil and simmer for 20 minutes. Remove from the heat, skim off any excess fat.
- Sieve the stock into a clean container and seal until required, throw away the vegetables and bones.

As Good as the Soups We Make...

The soups on the pages that follow are much like those we make in our own kitchen. Sure, our pots and pans may be a shade larger than yours, but essentially we make it the same way you do – by chopping, simmering and blending fresh, natural ingredients. It's all real, fresh soup whether you make it at home yourself or choose a New Covent Garden Food Company soup from the chiller cabinet in your local supermarket.

We don't put anything in our soups that you wouldn't have in your own kitchen – no flavourings, no preservatives, no gloopy, modified starches. It's fresh soup, exactly as we – and you – would expect to eat it at home or in a restaurant.

That's why we're the UK's favourite brand of fresh soup. Our soups taste as if you'd made them yourself and every bit as good as the soups in this recipe book.

Autumn

September, October & November

Autumn

The soup-cook's year starts here in the season of plenty. What you can't buy, you can gather for free: wild mushrooms, ripe blackberries, shiny chestnuts and wind-fallen apples. With the landowner's permission, the fruits of orchard, hedgerow and open field are yours for the taking.

Soup and surplus go together. These are the recipes that make the most of autumnal excess, the golden squashes, tart apples and tender carrots, plump pheasants and the first haul of new-season mussels.

With shortening days and abundant root vegetables, we cook for comfort as much as for pleasure. A shot of cream and a melting of mature cheese reflect our need for richness and satisfaction. Autumn soups are for camaraderie and for sharing – for retelling the events of an afternoon walk in leaf-strewn woods.

Mussel, White Wine & Garlic

You can tell from Alicia de la Torre's Spanish name that her roots – and her tastes – lie overseas. Although not typically Spanish, fresh mussels and garlic have been a staple of her diet for as long as she can remember; even now, mussels cooked in crisp white wine and garlic are still her favourite meal.

Our PR whirlwind, Alicia, volunteered to turn her favourite dish into an equally favourite soup for this book. The result looks and smells fantastic – a fragrant, sea-fresh, garlicky soup with a hint of chilli, and garnished with flat-leaf parsley and the first of the new season's shelled mussels.

Serves 4

Cooking time: 30 minutes

- 2 kg (4 ½ lb) mussels, cleaned
- 5 tablespoons olive oil
- 3 cloves garlic, finely chopped
- 370 ml (½ bottle) white wine
- 4 shallots, finely sliced
- 1 red chilli, finely chopped
- 120 ml (4 ¼ fl. oz) double cream
- 1 small bunch flat leaf parsley, finely chopped
- Salt and freshly ground black pepper

- Clean the mussels thoroughly under cold running water, scrubbing well to get rid of any barnacles and removing the mussel beards. Throw any away that are open or that have cracked shells. Change the water several times.
- Heat 2 tablespoons of the olive oil in a large, heavy-based pan. Add half the garlic and all of the mussels, cover and shake vigorously to coat the mussels with the oil. Add the wine, cover and cook for 2–3 minutes until the shells open.
- Pour the mussels and cooking juices into a large bowl to cool. Remove three-quarters of the mussels from their shells, discarding any that have not opened. Keep the cooking juices – you'll need those in a few minutes.
- Return the pan to the heat, add the remaining olive oil and garlic, the shallots and chilli, then cook for 5 minutes until golden.
- Add the cooking juices, cream and half the parsley, then reduce slightly to thicken.
- Add the cooked mussels and reheat for 5 minutes, stirring frequently.
- Season to taste. Add the remaining parsley and serve.

Trout & Watercress

The plump trout that Rebecca Pope (she sells our soups to the supermarkets) used to catch on her aunt and uncle's trout farm led her to look up every trout recipe she could find. Here, she teams it with crisp green watercress, a natural detoxifier and an obvious freshwater companion to trout.

Rebecca likes watercress because it cooks quickly, after which it blends to a beautifully smooth finish. She holds back the poached trout till the end to produce distinct yet complementary textures: a swirl of flaked fish within a luxuriously creamy base.

Decorate with a sprig of watercress for a special finish.

Cooking time: 1 hour

Serves 4

1 whole trout, filleted

565 ml (1 pint) fish stock

50 g (2 oz) butter

2 medium onions, finely chopped

2 medium potatoes, finely chopped

2 cloves garlic, crushed

1 litre (1 3/4 pints) vegetable stock

250 g (9 oz) watercress, hard stalks trimmed

Salt and freshly ground black pepper

- Poach the trout fillets in the fish stock for 5-10 minutes until cooked. Remove it from the stock, cool, discard the skin and bones, then flake the fish. Set aside.
- Melt the butter, add the onions, potato and garlic, cover and sweat for 10 minutes without colouring.
- Add the vegetable stock and bring to the boil. Add the watercress and bring back to the boil cooking for 5 minutes.
- Blend until smooth.
- Return the soup to the pan, season to taste, then gently cook for a further 2 minutes.
- Place the flaked trout in the serving bowl and pour soup over to serve.

Tomato, Fennel & Feta

Amanda Butterfield is the chef who can't stop fiddling with a recipe. We think we've got a recipe right, then she comes along and adjusts it. It would be infuriating if she weren't always right – which is just as infuriating.

In this recipe, we let her have her way from beginning to end. The subtle hint of aniseed and the soft nuggets of feta are an unexpected stroke of genius.

When you serve this to your guests, it will look and taste like a culinary masterpiece – exotic and comforting in equal measure. Don't spoil the effect by telling everyone that it was a doddle to make.

Serves 4

Cooking time: 65 minutes

- 1 tablespoon olive oil
- 1 fennel bulb, finely sliced
- 1 small potato, diced
- 1 tablespoon tomato purée
- 1 small onion, diced
- 1 clove garlic, finely chopped
- 1 teaspoon caster sugar
- 2 tablespoons white-wine vinegar
- 300 g (10½ oz) tomatoes, chopped
- 1 tablespoon sun-dried tomato paste
- 450 ml (16 fl.oz) water
- 50 g (2 oz) feta cheese, diced
- Salt and freshly ground black pepper

- Heat the olive oil in a pan, add part of the fennel (only 40 g/1½ oz at this stage), followed by the potato, tomato purée, onion and garlic. Cook for 8–10 minutes until the vegetables are soft and without too much colour.
- Add the sugar and white-wine vinegar, then reduce by half.
- Once reduced, add the chopped tomatoes and sun-dried tomato paste, then cook for a further 5 minutes.
- Add the water, cover and gently cook for a further 30 minutes.
- Blend until smooth.
- Once smooth, add the remaining fennel and feta cheese. Season to taste, cook gently for a further 10 minutes, then serve.

Mediterranean Vegetable & Tomato

If we told you that our accountant, Michael Kavanagh, gave us this recipe, you might be tempted to yawn and turn the page. That would be a mistake.

In an earlier life, he was a taut-muscled, sun-tanned beach bum who wandered round the Greek islands during his year after university. Michael's Greek-god looks may have faded, but his talent for Greek cooking remains.

This bright and chunky soup takes you straight back to those fragrant island hillsides. The colour comes from a mixture of sunny red and yellow peppers, courgettes and tomatoes, while smoked paprika, sun-dried-tomato paste and rosemary recall the leisurely alfresco meals of long-forgotten summers.

Serves 4

Cooking time: 30 minutes

1 tablespoon olive oil
1 small onion, finely chopped
1 clove garlic, crushed
½ red pepper, diced
½ yellow pepper, diced
2 courgettes, diced
1 teaspoon sweet smoked paprika
1 teaspoon fresh rosemary, finely chopped
1 teaspoon balsamic vinegar
400 g (14 ¼ oz) tin chopped tomatoes
1 litre (1 ¾ pints) vegetable stock
1 tablespoon sun-dried-tomato paste
1 teaspoon fresh parsley, finely chopped
Salt and freshly ground black pepper

- Heat the oil in a pan, add the onion and garlic, then gently cook for 5 minutes without colouring.
- Add the peppers, courgettes, paprika and rosemary, cook for 3 minutes, stirring constantly.
- Add the balsamic vinegar, simmer for 2 minutes, then add the chopped tomatoes and stock and bring to the boil.
- Reduce the heat, cover and simmer for 15 minutes until vegetables are tender.
- Stir in the sun-dried tomato paste and parsley, then season to taste and serve.

Spicy Chicken, Pea & Apricot

Harissa is a spicy, red sesame-seed paste with an aroma that conjures up crowded Moroccan markets and lonely desert tents. You'll find it in kitchens throughout North Africa – and in supermarkets throughout the UK.

It's just the kind of fiery and exotic ingredient that our Colin Wilson (he keeps our soup deliveries flowing) loves to experiment with. He has a soft spot for foods with a Middle Eastern feel.

Here, he's balanced the spiciness of the harissa with the sweetness of apricot, and rounded off with another Moroccan favourite, peas.

Serves 4   Cooking time: 30 minutes

1 tablespoon olive oil
1 small onion, finely chopped
1 clove garlic, crushed
750 ml (26 fl. oz) chicken stock
1 teaspoon Harissa paste
50 g (1¾ oz) rice, uncooked
75 g (3 oz) cooked chicken, diced
100 g (3½ oz) fresh peas
50 g (1¾ oz) dried apricots, diced
1 sprig fresh coriander, chopped
Salt and freshly ground black pepper

- Heat the oil in a pan, add the onion and garlic, then gently cook without colouring for 5 minutes.
- Add the stock and Harissa and bring to the boil, then reduce the heat to simmer gently.
- Add the rice and cook for 15 minutes.
- Add the cooked chicken, peas and apricots and continue to simmer for a further 10 minutes until the rice is cooked.
- Season to taste, garnish with fresh coriander and serve.

Beetroot, Raspberry & Sparkling Wine

Whenever we open the bubbly, our chef, Claire Francis, is first with her glass. By coincidence, she's the chef most likely to use fizz and sparkle to bring a soup to life.

Her inspiration for this recipe came from childhood memories of sweet, late-summer raspberries and red-staining beetroot on her granddad's allotment. That's where Claire developed her lifelong connection between food and fun. She often cooks with a glass of sparkling wine in one hand and plenty more in the saucepan – and always with a smile on her face.

Serves 4   Cooking time: 30 minutes

3 beetroots (250 g (9 oz)), cooked not pickled
1 small red onion, finely chopped
90 g (3 oz) fresh raspberries
1 tablespoon caster sugar
1 teaspoon red-wine vinegar
565 ml (1 pint) vegetable stock
2 tablespoons sparkling wine
Salt and freshly ground black pepper

- Place the beetroot, red onion, raspberries and sugar in a pan and heat gently until the raspberries and the beetroot start to colour the other ingredients.
- Add the red-wine vinegar, bring to the boil and reduce the liquid by half.
- Add the vegetable stock and bring to the boil. Once boiling, cover and simmer for 30 minutes until the beetroot starts to break down.
- Blend until smooth.
- Return to the pan, add the sparkling wine, then season to taste and serve.

Cream of Artichoke

This is a scrumptiously creamy dinner party treat that will get your guests talking, if only to discover how you made it.

Yes, spiky globe artichokes do take a little longer to prepare, but the results are worth it. Even if you take the quicker route and open a tin of artichoke hearts, the smooth sophistication of this soup will still confirm your position as a paid-up domestic goddess (or god, as the case may be).

Serves 4
Cooking time: 1 hour 20 minutes

1 tablespoon white-wine vinegar

4 (300g / 10½ oz) globe artichokes

850 ml (1½ pints) chicken stock

1 small onion, finely chopped

2 tablespoons fresh lemon juice

1 teaspoon thyme, chopped

105 ml (3½ fl. oz) single cream

Salt and freshly ground black pepper

- Fill a large bowl with 500ml water and add the white-wine vinegar.
- Trim the artichoke stems flush with the bottom of the artichoke so they sit flat. Slice off the top quarter of the artichoke and remove tips of leaves with a sharp knife. Remove the outer leaves and cut the artichoke into quarters.
- Place the artichoke quarters in the bowl of prepared water to prevent discoloration.
- With a small knife, remove the fuzzy centres, leaving the artichoke heart intact.
- Add the stock, prepared artichokes, onions, lemon juice and thyme to a large pan, bring to boil, cover and simmer for 30 minutes or until artichokes are tender.
- Drain the artichokes from the mixture and reserve the cooking liquor.
- Scrape the flesh from the base of each leaf and add to the artichoke hearts.
- Blend the artichoke flesh and cooking liquor until smooth.
- Return to the pan, add the cream and season to taste, heat gently for 3 minutes and serve. This soup is just as delicious served chilled.

Cauliflower & Vintage Cheddar

After a tough game of rugby, Mike Money likes nothing better than the simple, hearty comfort of cauliflower cheese. But Jessica, his wife and our head chef, prefers soup. So she came up with this post-match lifesaver that's even more comforting than the meal that inspired it.

Like all the recipes in this book, this one's easily adapted to suit your tastes and the contents of your fridge. Choose a different Cheddar, add your own seasonings (a shot of Worcestershire sauce perhaps?) *et, voilà*, you have your own secret recipe finished with a flourish of fresh shavings from your preferred Cheddar!

Serves 4

Cooking time: 30 minutes

25 g (1 oz) butter
1 small onion, finely chopped
1 medium potato, diced
1 medium cauliflower (300 g/10½ oz), small florets
500 ml (18 fl. oz) vegetable stock
150 ml (5 fl. oz) milk
100 g (3½ oz) vintage Cheddar, grated
Salt and freshly ground black pepper

- Melt the butter in a pan, then add the onion and potato cooking gently for 5 minutes, without colouring.
- Add the cauliflower and stock, bring to the boil, cover then simmer for 20 minutes until vegetables are tender.
- Blend until smooth.
- Return to the pan, on a gentle heat add the milk and cheddar cheese, stirring continuously until the cheese has melted – but don't allow it to boil.
- Season to taste and serve.

Roast Pumpkin & Bramley Apple

Cheerful, sunset-orange pumpkins and sharp, fat Bramley apples sum up the mood of autumn. It seems right to bring them together in a soup.

We'd like to claim the pairing as our own, but we can't. Sheina Smith, the mother of our marketing dynamo, Michelle Harriman, came up with the same idea years ago. She suggests roasting the pumpkins in olive oil to multiply the flavour and soften the flesh. By the time the apple and pumpkin come together, they're soft enough, she says, to cheer up the dampest of October evenings.

Serves 4

Cooking time: 1 hour

1 large pumpkin

2 tablespoons olive oil

25 g (1 oz) butter

1 small onion, finely chopped

670 ml (1¼ pints) chicken stock

1 small Bramley apple, finely diced, skin off

Salt and freshly ground black pepper

- **Preheat oven to 230°C/gas mark 8.**
- **Cut the pumpkin into quarters, scoop out seeds and discard.**
- **Brush flesh with olive oil and place in roasting tin; bake for 25 minutes until flesh is soft. Once cooled, scoop the flesh out of the skin.**
- **Melt the butter in a pan, add the onion, cover and cook for 10 minutes, without colouring.**
- **Add the stock and pumpkin flesh, cover and simmer gently for 15 minutes.**
- **Add the apple, cover and simmer for a further 5 minutes until tender.**
- **Blend a third of the soup until smooth.**
- **Return the blended soup to the pan, season to taste and stir well. Cook for a further 2 minutes and serve.**

Sweet Potato, Butternut Squash & Smoked Chilli

This sweet and creamy soup has a shot of smoky fire running through it. It's our hot-blooded chef Juliette Shaw's antidote to the shortening hours of daylight, although it may not be for the faint-hearted.

Juliette likes to raise the temperature when she cooks. In this case, the squash, cream and sweet potato offset the heat of the chilli, while the smoked paprika adds warmth and depth to its fire. This is one evening when you might want to turn down the central heating.

Serves 4

Cooking time: 50 minutes

25 g (1 oz) butter
1 clove garlic, crushed
225 g (8 oz) sweet potato, diced
1 small butternut squash, diced
¼ teaspoon sweet smoked paprika
½ red chilli, finely diced
750 ml (26 fl. oz) vegetable stock
2 teaspoons wholegrain mustard
1 tablespoon Parmesan cheese, finely grated
125 ml (¼ pint) double cream
Salt and freshly ground black pepper

- Melt the butter in a pan, add the garlic, sweet potato and butternut squash, stir, cover and cook for 10 minutes.
- Add the smoked paprika and red chilli, then cook for 1 minute.
- Add the stock and bring to the boil, cover and simmer for 15–20 minutes until vegetables are tender.
- Allow to cool a little, then stir in the mustard and Parmesan. Blend until smooth.
- Return to the pan, add the cream, season to taste, then gently reheat for 2 minutes and serve.

Pheasant & Roasted Shallot

Mark Glynne-Jones, from our design agency, likes to bag his soup ingredients on the wing. He shoots pheasant with his father in his native Cotswolds and subsequently turns his catch into soup.

This is the game soup he likes to come home to after a day in the country. It's big enough to stand up as a meal in its own right. The chunky flavour and texture come from the shredded pheasant breasts, while the sweet caramelized shallots are a perfect foil for the richness of the game and sherry. Garnish with chopped fresh parsley.

Serves 4

Cooking time: 1 hour 15 minutes

- 8 shallots, peeled
- 2 tablespoons olive oil
- 25 g (1 oz) butter
- 3 pheasant breasts
- 2 tablespoons dry sherry
- 1 large potato, diced
- 2 medium carrots, diced
- 565 ml (1 pint) chicken stock
- 2 tablespoons fresh thyme, chopped
- 1 tablespoon parsley, finely chopped
- Salt and freshly ground black pepper

- Preheat the oven to 190°C/gas mark 5
- Toss the shallots in 2 tablespoons of the olive oil and roast in the oven for 20 minutes until soft and caramelized.
- Heat the butter and remaining olive oil in a pan and seal the pheasant breasts on both sides.
- Add the sherry, bring to the boil, then simmer for 2 minutes. Add the potato and carrots then stir for 1 minute.
- Add the chicken stock, thyme and shallots, bring to the boil and simmer for a further 30 minutes. Remove the pheasant breasts and put them to one side to cool.
- Blend the liquor until smooth.
- Once the pheasant breasts are cooled, shred the meat using 2 forks.
- Return the soup to the pan, season to taste, add the meat and parsley, then reheat gently for 5 minutes and serve.

Sweet Potato & Red Pepper Chowder

A bowlful of sweet and spicy comfort is as much as anyone needs on a damp autumnal day. It warms you up after you've put the garden to bed for the winter; it draws the family round the fireside when the wind picks up.

We've made this soup cheerful and peppery. There's masses of colour, texture and heart-warming fire in the form of red peppers, sweetcorn and chilli – and a generous dollop of comfort in the form of double cream and sweet potato.

Serves 4

Cooking time: 40 minutes

1 tablespoon olive oil
1 small onion, finely diced
1 large sweet potato, diced
1 tablespoon plain flour
670 ml (1¼ pints) vegetable stock
125 g (4½ oz) sweetcorn kernels
½ red pepper, finely sliced
½ red chilli, finely diced
2 spring onions, finely sliced
4 tablespoons double cream
1 teaspoon parsley, finely chopped
Salt and freshly ground black pepper

- Heat the olive oil in a pan, add the onion and sweet potato, then sweat for 5 minutes without colouring.
- Add the flour and cook for 1 minute, then add the vegetable stock and bring to the boil. Cover and simmer for 15 minutes until tender.
- Blend until smooth.
- Return to the pan and add the sweetcorn, red pepper, chilli and spring onions, cover and simmer gently for 5 minutes to soften vegetables.
- Add the cream and parsley, then season to taste and serve.

Maple Roast Parsnip

Don't be tempted to treat this soup like a cocktail. 'Shaken, not stirred' doesn't apply, even though the recipe was devised by our very own James Bond, the man who sells our soups to local restaurants.

James's weapon of choice is the ladle, which he uses to turn a saucepan of bubbling ingredients into an exquisite treat. He adds a coating of maple syrup to sweet and earthy caramelized roast parsnips with divine results.

You could do the same. To finish the job, all you have to do is blend until smooth before stirring (not shaking!) with double cream.

Serves 4

Cooking time: 45 minutes

2 tablespoons olive oil
4 medium parsnips, cut into lengths
2 tablespoons maple syrup
25 g (1 oz) butter
1 medium onion, finely chopped
1 clove garlic, crushed
1 tablespoon plain flour
1 litre (1 3/4 pints) chicken stock
4 tablespoons double cream
Salt and freshly ground black pepper

- Preheat oven to 190°C/gas mark 5.
- Place the olive oil into a roasting dish, then heat in the oven.
- Steam the parsnips for 6 minutes until soft.
- Toss the steamed parsnips into the roasting dish and roast for 15 minutes until starting to colour. Add the maple syrup and roast for a further 10–15 minutes until sticky and caramelized.
- Remove the roasting dish from the oven and allow to cool.
- Meanwhile, melt the butter in a pan and cook the onions and garlic until soft. Add the flour, then cook for a further minute.
- Add the stock and roasted parsnips, bring to boil, cover and simmer for 10 minutes.
- Blend until smooth.
- Return to the pan, stir in the cream, then season to taste. Cook gently for a further 2 minutes and serve.

Bacon, Broccoli & Celeriac

Soup was high on Jeremy Hudson's list of dislikes when he was a child – he'd always be arguing with his dad about having to eat his speciality autumn soup.

But no one can fight the inevitable, and eventually, we all turn out like our parents. These days Jeremy, who's now our finance director, finds himself cooking the same soup his dad made – and enjoying every spoonful. He even uses the same ingredients: crispy dry-cured bacon and earthy celeriac, with broccoli and baby leaf spinach for an attractive green finish.

Like father, like son – like soup.

Serves 4   Cooking time: 45 minutes

1 tablespoon olive oil
4 rashers smoked dry cured bacon, diced
2 small onions, finely chopped
1 small celeriac, peeled and finely chopped
1 small broccoli, cut into small florets
700 ml (1¼ pints) vegetable stock
1 bay leaf
1 teaspoon thyme, finely chopped
1 teaspoon rosemary, finely chopped
100 g (3½ oz) baby leaf spinach
Salt and freshly ground black pepper

- Heat the olive oil in a pan, then fry the bacon until crispy. Remove and set aside.
- Fry the onions until soft, add the celeriac and broccoli, then cook for 5 minutes.
- Add the crispy bacon, vegetable stock and herbs and bring to the boil. Cover and simmer for 15–20 minutes until vegetables are tender.
- Remove the soup from the heat, add the spinach leaves, stirring the leaves in to wilt them.
- Blend until smooth, then return to the pan. Season to taste, reheat gently and serve.

Venison, Apple & Blackberry

There's still plenty of food out there for free – if you know where to look and what you're looking for. For beginners, blackberry picking is the place to start.
If you're like the family of our kitchen manager, Steve Johnson, you may even turn the hunt into a sticky, fun-filled day out that ends with a feast.

When the Johnsons get home, this is the soup they make. It's rich, dark and fruity – one of those chunky, can't-wait-to-get-stuck-in, casserole-style soups that double as meals.

Venison is superb with the apples and blackberries, but any red meat will work if you're in a hurry.

Serves 4

Cooking time: 50 minutes

- 15 g (½ oz) butter
- 60 g (2 oz) venison meat, cut into strips
- 1 small red onion, diced
- 1 small carrot, diced
- 1 leek, sliced
- 1 small potato, diced
- 1 small Bramley apple, diced
- 1 stick celery, diced
- 2 tablespoons red wine
- 1 tablespoon red wine vinegar
- 25 g (1 oz) brown sugar
- 15 g (½ oz) plain flour
- 80 g (3 oz) fresh blackberries
- 1 litre (1¾ pints) beef stock

- Melt the butter in a pan, add the venison meat and cook until lightly browned. Remove and set aside.
- Add the red onion, carrot, leek, potato, apple and celery to the pan, then cook until they start to brown.
- Add the red wine and red wine vinegar, bring to the boil, then reduce the liquid by half.
- Reduce the heat to simmer, add the sugar and flour, mixing in well.
- Add half of the blackberries and all the beef stock and bring to the boil. Once it is boiling, cover and simmer for 20 minutes until the vegetables are soft.
- Add the cooked venison and remaining blackberries, simmer for 5 minutes and serve.

Pumpkin & Scary Carrot

If we hadn't named this soup Pumpkin & Scary Carrot, we'd have had to call it Dan's Birthday Soup. Dan Gough's birthday (he's our brand manager) comes at th end of October, so birthday parties and Hallowe'en parties tend to be one and the same thing.

This is the simple themed soup he makes to keep birthday and Hallowe'en guests going throughout the night. Dan likes to serve it in a big tureen made from a hollowed-out, baked pumpkin. He garnishes it with scary(ish) cut-out carrot shapes.

But don't let that put you off – serving straight from the saucepan will do. The warmth, the golden colour and the gentle hint of nutmeg shine through, however you serve it.

Serves 4

Cooking time: 45 minutes

25 g (1 oz) butter

1 medium onion, finely chopped

1 medium pumpkin, chopped

2 large carrots, chopped

670 ml (1¼ pints) vegetable stock

125 ml (¼ pint) milk

Freshly grated nutmeg, to taste

1 carrot, cut into Hallowe'en shapes

Salt and freshly ground black pepper

- Melt the butter in a pan and cook the onion gently for 5 minutes without colouring.
- Add the pumpkin, carrots and vegetable stock, bring to the boil, then cover and simmer gently for 20 minutes until vegetables are tender.
- Blend until smooth.
- Return to the pan, add the milk, then the nutmeg to taste.
- Season to taste, then cook gently for a further 3 minutes, add the Hallowe'en carrot shapes and serve.

Simple Parsnip & Apple

Parsnips and Bramley apples grow in abundance in many a country garden. Luckily, they're the sort of soft, sweet and easy-to-blend ingredients that go together well.

With so much ripening at one time, it's not worth making soup in small quantities. So cook big with plenty of leftovers for the next day and lots more for the freezer. And, for added texture, garnish with grated apple.

Serves 4

Cooking time: 45 minutes

50 g (2 oz) butter

5 parsnips, peeled and cut into chunks

1 large Bramley apple, peeled and cut into chunks

1 litre (1³/4 pints) vegetable stock

600 ml (21 fl. oz) milk

Salt and freshly ground black pepper

- Melt the butter in a pan, add the parsnips and apple, cook for 5–10 minutes.
- Add the stock, cover and simmer for 20 minutes or until the parsnips are cooked.
- Remove from the heat and allow to cool for a few minutes.
- Add the milk – it may curdle, but don't worry.
- Blend until smooth, then return to the pan.
- Season to taste, reheat gently for 5 minutes, then serve.

Caramelized Root Vegetable

Root vegetables are at the heart of many soups. But here they're the stars of the show.

It doesn't take much work to give root veg a sweet caramelized lift. We added a spoonful of honey and cooked for a few minutes till they took on a golden glow. You could do the same with your own selection of vegetables – whatever you can dig from your garden or buy at your nearest farmers' market. However you play it, this soup will go down well with hungry kids.

Serves 4

Cooking time: 40 minutes

1 medium potato, diced

2 medium carrots, diced

1 small swede, diced

1 turnip, diced

1 leek, sliced

1 parsnip, diced

426 ml ($^3/_4$ pint) vegetable stock

25 g (1 oz) butter

1 tablespoon honey

Salt and freshly ground black pepper

- Place half of the potato, carrots and swede in a pan, followed by all of the turnip, leek, parsnip and vegetable stock.
- Bring to the boil, then cover and simmer for 20 minutes.
- Blend until smooth and keep to one side.
- Melt the butter in a pan (use the same one as before if you've blended in a bowl – anything to save washing up!), add the remaining potato, carrot and swede, then gently cook until lightly browned.
- Add the honey and allow to caramelise on a medium heat for 7 minutes.
- Add the blended soup, season to taste, then stir well and serve.

Beef, Ale & Wild Mushroom

Our mushroom-mad chef Chris Moxon and his wife Jo used to go mushrooming with an expert who supplied mushrooms to the Hampshire Hotel where Chris used to work.

Now Chris uses that knowledge to go foraging in the autumn woods. But he warns that, if you don't know what you're looking for, it's far safer to pick them up fresh or dried from your local supermarket. That way you can still make his favourite beefy, mushroom recipe.

Beef, Ale & Wild Mushroom is more like a Sunday roast than a soup. The rich and meaty flavour comes from long, slow cooking in ale, while the mixture of mushrooms gives a range of contrasting textures.

Serves 4   Cooking time: 1 hour 30 minutes

2 tablespoons olive oil
200 g (7 oz) braising steak, cut into thin slivers
1 medium red onion, small wedges
2 cloves garlic, crushed
1 tablespoon flour
284 ml (½ pint) ale
2 sprigs of thyme
565 ml (1 pint) beef stock
300 g (10½ oz) mushrooms (we used 100 g (3½ oz) of each: shiitake, oyster, button)
1 tablespoon redcurrant jelly
Salt and freshly ground black pepper

- Heat 1 tablespoon of the olive oil in a pan. Add the braising steak, cook until sealed and lightly coloured, remove and set aside.
- Add the remaining olive oil, red onion and garlic to the pan, then cook until lightly caramelized.
- Add the flour and cook for 1 minute, stirring all the time.
- Add the ale, thyme and stock and bring to the boil.
- Add the steak and mushrooms, cover and simmer gently for 1 hour 15 minutes.
- Add the redcurrant jelly, season to taste and serve.

Cock-a-Leekie

Harsh climates and sustaining soups go together. This creamy blend of chicken and leek has kept the Scottish winter at bay for generations.

We think Cock-a-Leekie makes a great starter. The flavours are simple (as is the cooking) and the mood is upbeat. Serve it with crusty rolls and you'll soon have your guests tearing and dipping and talking like old friends.

Serves 4

Cooking time: 45 minutes

1 leek, sliced

1 medium potato, diced

1 small onion, chopped

565 ml (1 pint) chicken stock

130 g chicken, cooked and diced

1 teaspoon parsley, chopped

2 tablespoons double cream

Salt and freshly ground black pepper

- Place half of the leek and potato in a pan, add all of the onion and chicken stock, then bring to the boil. Cover and simmer for 25 minutes.
- Blend until smooth.
- Return to the pan, add the remaining leek and potato, then cook for 15 minutes until soft.
- Add the cooked chicken and fresh parsley.
- Add the cream, season to taste and stir. Cook for a further 5 minutes and serve.

Cullen Skink

How is it that such a tasty soup has such an uninviting name? Cullen is a village on the southern shores of the Moray Firth, and skink comes from the German word for ham. But meat has long since disappeared from this traditional Scottish fish and potato soup.

So don't be put off by the name, this is one soup you must try. The flavours of smoked haddock, parsley and potato blend without effort, while the textures of flaked fish and creamy smooth potato are hearty enough to withstand a North Sea gale.

Serves 4

Cooking time: 45 minutes

- 100 ml (3½ fl. oz) whole fat milk
- 426 ml (¾ pint) vegetable stock
- 2 fillets smoked haddock
- 25 g (1 oz) butter
- 1 small onion
- 1 medium potato, diced
- 1 teaspoon parsley, chopped
- 2 tablespoons double cream
- Salt and freshly ground black pepper

- Heat the milk and half of the vegetable stock in a pan. Add the smoked haddock and poach for 10 minutes until lightly cooked.
- Remove from the heat and cool the fish in the liquid.
- In another pan, melt the butter, add the onion and cook gently for 5 minutes without colouring.
- Add the potato and the remaining vegetable stock, then bring to the boil. Cover and simmer for 15 minutes until the potato is soft.
- Add the liquid from the poached haddock to the pan, but not the fish.
- Blend until smooth, return to the pan. Add the smoked haddock, chopped parsley and heat gently for 2 minutes.
- Add the double cream, season to taste and serve.

Pear, Roquefort & Spinach

Here's a dinner party sensation that's ready in less time than it takes to say Per (pronounced 'pear') Hogberg. OK, well not quite that quick – but *pretty* quick.

Per is our supermarket salesman. With his Swedish roots, he takes a slightly different approach to soups and what you should put in them. Pear (pronounced 'Per'!), Roquefort & Spinach is a superb example based on mouthwatering ingredients.

Roquefort is a prince of cheeses – crumbly and creamy with a sweet blue tang; pear is fresh and tart; while dark-green spinach has a delicate hint of bitterness. Together they're sublime – soft nuggets of melting cheese in a sea of green.

Serves 4

Cooking time: 30 minutes

50 g (2 oz) butter

1 large onion, finely chopped

1 large potato, finely chopped

2 cloves garlic, crushed

750 ml (26 fl. oz) water

250 g (9 oz) spinach

2 pears, diced

50 g (2 oz) Roquefort cheese, diced

Salt and freshly ground black pepper

- Melt the butter in a pan, add the onion, potato and garlic. Cover and cook gently for 10 minutes without colouring.
- Add the water and bring to the boil. Add the spinach, bring back to the boil, then cook for 5 minutes.
- Blend until smooth and return to the pan.
- Blend the pears until smooth, then add to blended soup, stir in well.
- Add the Roquefort cheese and season to taste. Heat gently for 3 minutes and serve.

Honey-Glazed Chantenay Carrot

The 18-year success story of our best-selling Carrot & Coriander inspired our inquisitive food sleuth, Amanda Jackson-Piggot, to track down the ultimate carrot soup. The hunt's not over yet, although this recipe comes pretty close.

Amanda suggested baby Chantenay carrots for their sweet and tender flavour, and her favourite acacia honey for the glaze. The other ingredients are as simple as you can get. Their job is to let the essential carrotyness shine through. It certainly does.

Serves 4

Cooking time: 45 minutes

- 400 g (13 oz) Chantenay carrots, top and tailed
- 50 g (2 oz) butter
- 1 medium potato, diced
- 1 medium onion, diced
- 3 tablespoons Acacia honey
- 700 ml (1¼ pints) vegetable stock
- Salt and freshly ground black pepper

- Top and tail the carrots, then boil for 20 minutes until *al dente*.
- Melt half of the butter in a pan, add the potato and onion, cover and cook gently for 10 minutes without colouring.
- Drain the carrots, return them to their pan, melt the remaining butter over the top, then add the honey.
- Heat, stirring frequently, until the liquid is reduced and lightly coloured.
- Add the stock to the carrot pan, stirring well, then add the cooked potato and onion.
- Bring to the boil, cover and simmer for 20 minutes.
- Blend until smooth.
- Return to the pan and season to taste. Heat gently for 2 minutes and serve.

Bangers & Beans

Hands up who likes sausage and beans! Just about everyone – including Sue Evans (our technical manager), whose *two* raised hands are flapping around like carrot tops in a gale. Sue loves Bangers & Beans so much that she turned them into a soup to prove her point.

Ever since, Bangers & Beans has been our Bonfire Night staple. It's chunky, rich, glossy, fragrant and smoky-sweet. In short, it has everything you need for a chilly evening in the open air.

Oh, and kids love it, too.

Serves 4
Cooking time: 1 hour 15 minutes

1 tablespoon olive oil
6 sausages, each cut into 6 pieces
1 small red onion, finely chopped
1 teaspoon sweet smoked paprika
2 tablespoons red wine
1 medium potato, diced
410 g tinned haricot beans
2 carrots, diced
1 litre (1¾ pints) beef stock
565 ml (1 pint) tomato passata
1 teaspoon oregano
Worcestershire sauce, to taste
Salt and freshly ground black pepper
1 tablespoon fresh parsley, chopped

- Heat the oil in large pan and fry the sausage pieces on all sides to brown. Remove from pan and set aside.
- Add the red onion to the pan and cook gently for 5 minutes.
- Add the paprika and red wine, then cook for a further minute.
- Add the potato, haricot beans, carrots, stock, passata and oregano.
- Bring to the boil, add the sausages, then cover and simmer gently for 30 minutes until vegetables are tender.
- Add to your liking the Worcestershire sauce, then season with salt and pepper to taste.
- Sprinkle with the chopped parsley and serve.

Winter

December, January & February

Winter

Nature rests, but it never sleeps. There's fresh food aplenty for those who look: in the stormy seas and crisp, blue skies, and rooted deep in protective winter soils.

The finest winter soups draw turbot from the ocean, duck from the wing and beef from the field. And from the gardeners' larder, full of turnip, swede and parsnip, come dozens of smooth and hearty blends, while frost-hardy sprouts and early cabbage add a splash of green colour.

These are the soups that see us through bitter nights and glittering parties. We celebrate quiet family evenings with nuggets of melted Stilton in steaming bowls of spinach and white wine; we introduce our smartest guests to the molten gold of champagne and Camembert. And, when we venture out for a walk in the snow, we take a warming flask of butternut squash tinged with ginger.

Jerusalem Artichoke & Porcini Mushroom

Our annual Create A Soup competition is a constant reminder that anyone can create fabulous soups. This smooth and sophisticated recipe was a worthy runner-up in 2003.

A little dried porcini goes a long way. Its intense flavour complements the nutty taste of Jerusalem artichoke, a root vegetable that comes from South America – and has no connection with either Jerusalem or artichokes.

Those two ingredients would probably make a fine soup on their own, but our Create A Soup entrant went further, adding bacon and double cream to win the judges over.

Serves 4

Cooking time: 45 minutes

25 g (1 oz) porcini mushrooms, dried
25 g (1 oz) unsalted butter
1 small onion, diced
1 clove garlic, chopped
100 g (3½ oz) bacon lardons
150 g (5 oz) mushrooms, sliced
8 Jerusalem artichokes, peeled and diced
360 ml (13 fl. oz) vegetable stock
2 tablespoons double cream
1 teaspoon parsley, chopped
Salt and freshly ground black pepper

- Soak the dried porcini mushrooms in enough hot water to cover them and leave overnight.
- Melt the butter in a pan, add the onion, garlic and bacon lardons. Cook for 5 minutes or until lightly browned.
- Add the sliced mushrooms to the pan, then cook for a further 5 minutes.
- Add the Jerusalem artichokes and cook for 3 minutes.
- Drain the porcini mushrooms and add them to the pan along with the vegetable stock, cover and cook for 30 minutes.
- Blend until smooth.
- Return to the pan, add the cream and parsley, then season to taste. Reheat gently for 3 minutes and serve.

Duck & Pomegranate

The seeds of pomegranate are red and jewel-like. So we like to sprinkle them into our Duck & Pomegranate soup and let their sparkle brighten the darkest days of the year.

This is a show-off dish with an Asian twist. The duck and mushrooms provide texture, while the tamari (a Japanese form of soy sauce) and pomegranate molasses (a thick, sweet syrup made from reduced pomegranate juice) create a richer sweet-and-sour flavour. Serve it to December guests and wait for their applause.

Look for tamari and pomegranate molasses in delis and specialist areas of supermarkets.

Serves 4   Cooking time: 1 hour 30 minutes

2 duck legs
2 teaspoons dried mushrooms
1 pomegranate
1 litre (1³/₄ pints) chicken stock
2 tablespoons tamari
2 teaspoons pomegranate molasses
3 spring onions
Salt and freshly ground black pepper

- Preheat oven to 200°C/gas mark 6.
- Season the duck legs and roast on a rack for 40 minutes. Allow to cool slightly but, while they're still warm, remove the meat from the skin and bones, then shred using two forks.
- Soak the dried mushrooms in a cup of freshly boiled water for 30 minutes.
- Cut the pomegranate in half, juice one half and remove the seeds from the other half. To remove the seeds, hold the pomegranate cut side down in one hand over a board and bash the skin of the pomegranate with a wooden spoon all over. The seeds will fall away from the pith.
- Heat the stock in a pan, add the duck meat, soaked mushrooms and water, pomegranate juice, tamari and pomegranate molasses. Bring to the boil and simmer gently for 5 minutes.
- Add the pomegranate seeds and spring onions, then season to taste. Continue to heat for a further 2 minutes and serve.

Cream of Celeriac & Truffle

Our best soup inventor, Stacey Howe, picks up many of her recipe ideas while dining at smart restaurants. Research, she calls it; living the high life at someone else's expense, more like! Still, she does come back with a notebook packed with ideas.

This is her interpretation of one memorably expensive night out. It's rich, creamy, smooth and indulgent – and perfect for a festive dinner party. The irresistible aromas of truffle and thyme suggest hours in the kitchen; you and we know better.

Serves 4

Cooking time: 40 minutes

25 g (1 oz) butter
1 tablespoon olive oil
1 medium celeriac, finely diced
1 large potato, finely diced
1 small onion, finely chopped
850 ml (1½ pints) vegetable stock
A few sprigs fresh thyme
3 tablespoons double cream
½ teaspoon truffle oil
Salt and freshly ground black pepper

- Melt the butter and olive oil in a pan, add the celeriac, potato and onion. Cover and gently cook for 10 minutes, until they begin to soften.
- Add the stock and thyme, cover and simmer for 20–30 minutes until the vegetables are tender.
- Blend until smooth.
- Return to the pan, gently add the cream and truffle oil.
- Season to taste, then heat gently for a further 5 minutes and serve.

Brussel Sprout & Gammon

Our receptionist and resident sprout enthusiast, Cari-Lynn Chapman, gave us this recipe for using up leftover sprouts. And, since Cari-Lynn never likes to waste anything, she creates a stock from the gammon before she pops it into the soup. If that seems like hard work, use the vegetable stock in the recipe below.

To make Cari-Lynn's stock, you should boil the gammon twice. Throw away the water from the first boiling because it'll be far too salty. Add the stock from the second boiling to your soup – but sparingly to keep the saltiness down.

Either way, this is a big-flavoured soup filled with chunks of sprout and gammon.

Serves 4
Cooking time: 40 minutes

50 g (2 oz) butter
1 clove garlic, crushed
1 small onion, finely chopped
300 g (10½ oz) Brussel sprouts, finely sliced (reserving 8 whole sprouts)
25 g (1 oz) whole roasted and peeled chestnuts, chopped
400 ml (14½ fl. oz) vegetable stock
200 g (7 oz) gammon, cooked and shredded
400 ml (14½ fl. oz) water
6 tablespoons single cream
Salt and freshly ground black pepper

- Melt the butter in a pan, add the garlic and onion, then cook gently for 5 minutes, or until softened.
- Add the sprouts and chestnuts and cook for a further 5 minutes without colouring.
- Add the stock and 150 g (5 oz) of the gammon and boil rapidly, uncovered, until the stock has reduced by half and the sprouts are just tender.
- Blend until smooth, adding a little of the water if required.
- Return to the pan, add the remaining water and cream, season to taste, then reheat gently for 5 minutes.
- Meanwhile, take the remaining sprouts, cut into quarters and cook in boiling water until *al dente*.
- Place the remaining shredded gammon in the middle of the serving bowl, ladle over the soup, garnish with the sprouts and serve.

Carrot & Ginger

If you like our famous Carrot & Coriander, you'll love this simpler – and slightly spicier – version. It comes from our own Kerry Wainwright, who sells our soups to the supermarkets, but who doesn't like to spend as long in the kitchen as the rest of us.

In fact, this recipe couldn't be easier or more versatile. You can add a little water at the end to thin the consistency or, for a richer treat, stir in a generous dollop of cream.

Serves 4

Cooking time: 35 minutes

1 tablespoon olive oil

1 small onion, diced

8 medium carrots, diced

1 teaspoon ginger, puréed

500 ml (18 fl. oz) chicken stock

Salt & freshly ground black pepper

- Heat the olive oil in a pan, add the onion and cook gently for 5 minutes without colouring.
- Add the carrots, ginger and stock. Bring to the boil, cover and simmer for 20 minutes until the carrots are soft.
- Blend until smooth.
- Return to the pan and season to taste. Add a little water at this stage if you want to thin the soup to your taste, then serve.

Leftover Soup

There is a recipe on this page, but the real message of this soup is: anything goes. That's the approach that David Parrott (dad of our marketing director, Nigel) takes. His post-Christmas Leftover Soup comes out different every time. The two constants are that he always packs it in a flask for a Boxing Day walk, and it always tastes fabulous.

David suggests making your stock from the turkey carcass and adjusting everything else to match what's in the fridge. 'Use it or lose it,' he says with fatherly practicality.

Serves 4

Cooking time: 50 minutes

25 g (1 oz) butter
2 medium potatoes, diced
1 small onion, finely chopped
1 clove garlic, crushed
½ small swede, diced
725 ml (1¼ pints) turkey or chicken stock
1 teaspoon fresh thyme, finely chopped
1 bay leaf
100 g (3½ oz) Brussel sprouts, whole
8 shallots, whole
2 tablespoons olive oil
2 parsnips, cut into eighths
2 carrots, cut into eighths
1 teaspoon fresh rosemary, finely chopped
Salt and freshly ground black pepper

- Preheat oven to 190°C/gas mark 5.
- Heat the butter in a pan, add the potatoes, onion, garlic and swede.
- Cover and cook gently for 10 minutes without colouring.
- Add the stock, thyme and bay leaf, then cover and simmer for 15 minutes.
- Add the sprouts and continue to cook until they are tender.
- Blend until smooth.
- Meanwhile, plunge the shallots into boiling water for 2–3 minutes, then soak in cold water to allow skins to slip off easily.
- Heat the oil in a roasting pan, add the parsnips, carrots and whole shallots, toss in the oil and sprinkle with the rosemary.
- Roast for 20 minutes until cooked and lightly caramelized.
- Return the blended soup to the pan, add the roasted parsnip, carrots and shallots then season to taste. Reheat gently for 5 minutes and serve.

Parsnip, Apple & Chestnut

The discovery of slices of roast chestnut in this creamy smooth soup never fails to raise a festive smile. It's a reminder that you can do anything with soup and that imagination often beats experience.

The idea for Parsnip, Apple & Chestnut came from Alex Tompkins, the man who buys our ingredients from the farmers and growers. It came to him in an idle moment. He tried it, it worked, and the other ingredients slipped naturally into place. For sheer comfort, there's no other soup to beat this combination of midwinter flavour and fireside cosiness.

Serves 4

Cooking time: 50 minutes

50 g (2 oz) butter

3 parsnips, diced

1 medium potato, diced

1 small onion, finely chopped

1.2 litres (2 pints) vegetable stock

1 medium Braeburn apple, peeled and diced

1 teaspoon fresh rosemary, finely chopped

3 tablespoons single cream

Salt and freshly ground black pepper

75 g (3 oz) whole chestnuts, roasted, peeled and finely sliced

- Melt half the butter in a pan, add the parsnips, potato and onion, then cover and cook gently for 10 minutes, or until they begin to soften.
- Add the stock, apple and rosemary, cover, then simmer for a further 20 minutes until the vegetables are tender.
- Blend until smooth.
- Return to the pan, add the cream, season to taste, then reheat gently for 5 minutes.
- Meanwhile, melt the remaining butter in a pan, add the roasted chestnuts, season and fry for 3–4 minutes until they are lightly coloured, ensuring the butter does not burn.
- Spoon the chestnuts into the centre of the serving bowl, ladle the soup over and serve.

Christmas Dinner Soup

You really can have too much of a good thing: Christmas dinner with both sets of in-laws, plus another dinner that you cook at home for yourself. Try this instead: a creamy turkey soup stuffed with all your Christmas favourites for a fraction of the time and effort.

The dried cranberries and ready-made stuffing aren't just timesavers: they add texture and taste – fruity bites and a crisp golden crunch.

It's festive, it's fun – and it makes a splendid lunch or evening snack.

Cooking time: 1 hour

Serves 4
200 g (7 oz) ready-made stuffing
15 g (½ oz) dried cranberries
25 g (1 oz) butter
1 leek, finely sliced
1 stick celery, finely chopped
1 small onion, finely chopped
750 ml (26 fl. oz) chicken stock
1 bay leaf
A few sprigs fresh thyme
100 ml (3½ fl. oz) single cream
200 g (7 oz) cooked turkey, diced
Salt and freshly ground black pepper

- Preheat oven to 190°C/gas mark 5.
- Roll the stuffing into 12 balls, then cook in the oven for approximately 20 minutes, until golden brown. Remove and keep to one side.
- Soak the dried cranberries in a cup of boiling water for 15 minutes, then drain and put to one side.
- Melt the butter in a pan, add the leek, celery and onion, then cook for 5 minutes, or until softened.
- Add the stock, bay leaf and thyme, cover and simmer for 20 minutes until the vegetables are tender.
- Remove the herbs and blend until smooth.
- Return to the pan, add the cream, turkey and cranberries, then season to taste. Reheat gently for 10 minutes, stirring occasionally.
- Place the stuffing balls in the centre of the serving bowl, ladle the soup over and serve.

New Year Root Vegetable

New Year resolutions start here: eat more fresh vegetables or, better still, eat more fresh soup.

This root-vegetable soup (a January 2006 Soup of the Month) is anything but bland. There's a hint of fire in the chilli and cumin, a comforting sweetness in the carrot and parsnip and a refreshing vigour in the leek and celery.

Our tip: eat a bowl of New Year Root Vegetable *before* you tackle the new season's holiday brochures.

Serves 4

Cooking time: 50 minutes

2 tablespoons olive oil

1 parsnip, diced

1 sweet potato, diced

2 small carrots, diced

1 small red onion, diced

1 leek, sliced

2 sticks celery, diced

445 ml ($^3/_4$ pint) water

1 teaspoon ground cumin

$^1/_2$ fresh red chilli, sliced

Salt & freshly ground black pepper

- Heat the olive oil in a pan, add the parsnip, sweet potato, carrots, red onion, leek and celery, then cook for 5 minutes until the vegetables have a little colour.
- Add the water, bring to the boil, cover and cook for 20 minutes or until the vegetables are soft.
- Blend until smooth.
- Return to the pan, add the cumin and chilli, then season to taste. Simmer for a further 10 minutes and serve.

Cauliflower, Mustard & Gorgonzola Cheese

Katie Rowen works at our PR agency, and is a big fan of soups. She gave us this recipe after she returned from a recent ski trip to Val d'Isère. Her soup was a spur-of-the-moment thing to satisfy a party of tired and hungry skiers. To her surprise, they insisted she make it again the following evening.

We can see why. Katie's soup is a smooth bowl of upmarket comfort. The shot of wholegrain mustard and the tang of Gorgonzola melt with ease into the wintry flavour of cauliflower.

For a bigger blue-cheese kick, choose a stronger, more mature Gorgonzola, and crumble in a few extra chunks just before serving.

Serves 4

Cooking time: 40 minutes

- 2 tablespoons vegetable oil
- 1 medium onion, finely chopped
- 1 tablespoon plain flour
- 284 ml (½ pint) vegetable stock
- 284 ml (½ pint) milk
- 1 medium cauliflower, cut into small florets
- 160 g (5½ oz) Gorgonzola cheese, cubed
- 1 teaspoon wholegrain mustard
- Salt and freshly ground black pepper

- Heat the oil in a pan, add the onion and cook without colouring, until softened. Add the flour and cook for 1 minute.
- Gradually add the stock and milk, stirring constantly.
- Add the cauliflower, bring to the boil, then cover and simmer for 20 minutes until the cauliflower is tender.
- Remove from the heat, add the Gorgonzola cheese, then stir until melted.
- Blend until smooth.
- Return to the pan, season to taste, then reheat gently for 3 minutes. Stir in the mustard and serve.

Spicy Mussels

The fresh, barnacle-covered mussels that our chef, Ross Chamberlain, buys from Morston in Norfolk are a pleasure to cook and eat. When he's at home with old friends he steams them in a gutsy Thai style with curry powder, coconut cream, coriander and lime juice.

This is a great gather-round-the-table sort of soup for a night in with a few bottles of beer. It's chunky and zesty and it keeps everyone talking long after they've discarded the last empty mussel shell.

Cooking time: 45 minutes

Serves 4

160 g (5½ oz) fresh mussels
1 small onion, diced
1 tablespoon vegetable oil
25 g (1 oz) unsalted butter
1 teaspoon curry powder
1 tablespoon plain flour
610 ml (22 fl. oz) fish stock
4 tablespoons double cream
40 g (1½ oz) coconut cream
1 teaspoon coriander, fresh
1 tablespoon lime juice
Salt & freshly ground black pepper

- Clean the mussels thoroughly under cold running water, scrubbing well to get rid of any barnacles and removing the mussel beards. Throw any away that are open or that have cracked shells. Change the water several times.
- Place the mussels in a pan with half the chopped onion and a little water (approximately 1 cm/½ inch), steam for 5 minutes until the mussels are open.
- Remove the mussels from the liquid and set to one side to cool, reserving the liquid for later. When cool, remove the mussels from their shells and leave to one side.
- Heat the oil and butter in a pan, add the remaining onion and the curry powder. Cook for 2 minutes to release the flavours, taking care not to burn the ingredients.
- Add the flour and stir in well for 1 minute. Add the fish stock and the liquid from cooking the mussels, stirring at all times and cook gently for 10 minutes, until thickened.
- Add the double cream and coconut cream, then simmer for 2 minutes.
- Blend until smooth.
- Return to the heat, add the mussels, coriander and lime juice, then season to taste. Heat gently for a further 3 minutes and serve.

Mushroom, Stilton & White Wine

Mushroom soup is as varied as the cooks who make it. Oliver Lewis-Barclay likes his bold and punchy (he's from our advertising agency, if you hadn't guessed!) so he blends his mushrooms with Stilton, a cheese that seems to belong in winter soups. They make a good pairing, made even more appetizing when cooked with bay leaf, garlic and a generous glug of white wine.

This is a smooth, creamy and luxurious soup finished with slivers of lightly sautéed mushrooms and chopped parsley.

Serves 4   Cooking time: 50 minutes

50 g (2 oz) butter
1 large onion, finely chopped
1 clove garlic, crushed
400 g (13 oz) closed cap mushrooms, sliced
700 ml (1¼ pints) vegetable stock
1 bay leaf
100 g (3½ oz) Stilton cheese, crumbled
1 tablespoon fresh parsley, chopped
200 ml (7½ fl. oz) white wine
3 tablespoons double cream
Salt & freshly ground black pepper

- Melt half the butter in a pan, add the onion and garlic and cook without colouring until softened.
- Add two-thirds (275 g/10 oz) of the mushrooms, all of the stock and the bay leaf, then bring to the boil. Cover and simmer for 20 minutes, stirring occasionally.
- Remove from the heat, add the cheese and half the parsley, then stir until melted.
- Blend until smooth.
- Meanwhile, melt the remaining butter in a frying pan, fry the remaining mushrooms for 5 minutes until lightly coloured, add the remaining parsley and leave to one side.
- Return blended soup to the pan, add the wine and cream, then season to taste.
- Reheat gently for 5 minutes. Add the fried mushrooms and serve.

Champagne & Camembert

Ripe Camembert has a luxurious texture that melts into soup. Champagne (or sparkling wine) suggests a celebration with every playful bubble. Between them, they make a velvety dinner-party dish that tastes as if it took all day to prepare.

No wonder Alan Moodie (one of our designers) suggested this recipe. He likes to eat well, but he doesn't want to spend all day in the kitchen. He says that Champagne & Camembert is the kind of soup that your guests will still be discussing when you serve the coffee and petits fours. Which is about twice as long as it took to make.

Serves 4   Cooking time: 40 minutes

120 g (4½ oz) ripe Camembert, diced

1 small knob butter

1 tablespoons olive oil

1 clove garlic, crushed

100 g (3½ oz) shallots, finely chopped

1 small potato, finely diced

225 ml (8 fl. oz) champagne

565 ml (1 pint) chicken stock

6 tablespoons single cream

Salt & freshly ground black pepper

- Make sure the Camembert is at room temperature. If it is not ripe, simply remove the skin, because this will not melt in your soup.
- Melt the butter and olive oil in a pan, add the garlic, shallots and potato, then cook without colouring until softened.
- Pour in the champagne. After 1 minute add the stock and bring to the boil. Cover and simmer for 20 minutes, stirring occasionally until the potato has broken down.
- Add the Camembert and allow it to melt over a low heat, stirring gently.
- Add the cream, season to taste, then heat gently for 2–3 minutes and serve.

Purple Sprouting Broccoli & Leek

The person with the happy job of reading the kind letters you send us is Debbie Bonnington. She's our Bridget Jones – single, big pants, Chardonnay by the bucketload – and she's been having a fling with purple sprouting broccoli.

Debbie's taken this soup vegetable to her heart, paired it with leek and added an unexpected twist of her own. She fried a few shreds of leek till they were caramelized and crispy, then tossed them in as a garnish. And not a hint of blue string anywhere!

Serves 4

Cooking time: 40 minutes

50 g (2 oz) butter

2 medium potatoes, diced

3 leeks, finely sliced

845 ml (1½ pints) vegetable stock

200 g (7 oz) purple sprouting broccoli

200 ml (7 fl. oz) milk

Salt & freshly ground black pepper

- Melt half the butter in a pan, add the potatoes and 2 of the leeks. Cover and cook for 10 minutes without colouring until softened.
- Add the stock, bring to the boil, then cover and simmer for 15 minutes.
- Add the broccoli and cook for a further 8–10 minutes until the broccoli is tender.
- Blend until smooth.
- Return to the pan, add the milk, season to taste and reheat gently.
- Meanwhile, melt the remaining butter in a frying pan and fry the remaining leeks until lightly caramelized.
- Ladle the soup into bowls, sprinkle the crispy leeks over the top and serve.

Haggis, Neeps & Tatties

Rob Burnett is our managing director and resident Scot. He loves the ritual of Burns Night and its plates of haggis with neeps and tatties. To prove his point to a sceptical audience, he turned the traditional Burns supper into a soup.

We were won over. There's enough meaty flavour in this chunky, whisky-tinged soup to justify a chorus of 'Auld Lang Syne'.

By the way, the vegetable that the Scots describe as a neep, or a turnip, is known as a swede in England, and vice versa.

Serves 4

Cooking time: 45 minutes

Half (250 g / 9oz) small haggis

25 g (1 oz) butter

3 small shallots, finely chopped

2 medium potatoes, diced

1 small swede, diced

425 ml ($^3/_4$ pint) vegetable stock

Salt & freshly ground black pepper

1 tablespoon fresh parsley, chopped

3 tablespoons whisky

- Remove the haggis from its packaging, wrap the required half in foil, then simmer in a pan for 40 minutes, or cook according to instructions on pack.
- Melt the butter in a pan, add the shallots, then cook without colouring until softened.
- Add the potatoes, swede and stock to the pan, bring to the boil, then cover. Simmer gently for 30 minutes until the vegetables are tender. Season to taste.
- Remove the haggis from its pan, then remove the foil. Divide across the serving bowls, creating small piles in the centres.
- Ladle the soup into the bowls, sprinkle with the parsley and a splash of whisky and serve.

Pak Choi & Chilli

Our cooking took a decidedly Eastern turn when Indonesian student Eva Tanudjaja joined us for six months' work experience. This was one of the first soups she showed us, and it remains our favourite.

Eva's style is fresh and invigorating. The crisp flavours of green vegetables contrast with the warmth of the ginger and heat of the fresh chilli. You don't just *think* this soup is doing you good: you can *feel* it doing good.

It's colourful, too – the brightest start we can offer to a healthy new year.

Serves 4 — **Cooking time: 40 minutes**

200 g (7 oz) pak choi, sliced
70 g (2½ oz) broccoli, small florets
½ fresh red chilli, chopped
1 teaspoon ginger purée
1 medium potato, diced
1 small onion, finely chopped
1 clove garlic, chopped
1 leek, finely sliced
50 g (1¾ oz) spinach, chopped
2 teaspoons demerara sugar
1 stick celery, chopped
565ml (1 pint) water
½ red pepper, sliced
Salt & freshly ground black pepper

- Place the pak choi (175 g/6 oz only at this stage), broccoli, chilli, ginger, potato, onion, garlic, leek, spinach, sugar, celery and water in a pan and bring to the boil.
- Once boiling, cover and simmer for 20 minutes or until all the vegetables are soft.
- Blend until smooth.
- Return to the pan, add the remaining pak choi and red pepper, then season to taste. Cook gently for a further 7 minutes and serve.

Oyster, Tomato & Saffron

Food plays as big a part in the chemistry of love as timing and location. And for sheer romance, nothing beats the chunky, mouthwatering appeal of oysters, prawns and turbot. To spoil someone rotten on Valentine's Day, spoon them this warm, saffron-tinged seafood extravaganza.

Cooking is brief, so, if you prepare everything in advance, you can devote oodles of time to the one you love.

Serves 4

Cooking time: 30 minutes

- 3 tablespoons olive oil
- 3 cloves garlic, crushed
- ½ red onion, chopped
- ½ bulb fennel, finely sliced
- ½ leek, chopped
- 725ml (1¼ pints) fish stock
- 200 g (7 oz) chopped tomatoes
- 200 g (7 oz) tomato passata
- Generous pinch saffron strands, soaked in 2 tablespoons hot water
- ½ red chilli, finely diced
- Few sprigs thyme
- 1 bay leaf
- ½ orange, zest of
- 3 tablespoons fresh parsley, chopped
- 250 g (9 oz) turbot or other white fish, filleted, large chunks
- 12 oysters, shelled
- 12 large raw prawns, shelled
- Salt and freshly ground black pepper

- Heat the oil in a pan, add the garlic, red onion, fennel and leek. Fry over a moderate heat, stirring frequently for 5–10 minutes until softened.
- Add the stock, chopped tomatoes, passata, soaked saffron, chilli, thyme, bay leaf, orange zest and 2 tablespoons of the parsley and bring to boil. Simmer on a moderate heat uncovered for 15 minutes.
- Add the turbot and cook gently for 5 minutes. Add the oysters with their juice and prawns and cook for a further 3–5 minutes until all the fish is cooked.
- Season to taste, sprinkle with the remaining parsley and serve.

Butternut Squash, Orange & Ginger

Here's colour and gentle, spicy warmth to enliven the dull days of February. Better still, this lovely golden soup is almost effortless. Ground ginger and ready-made orange juice shorten the preparation time, while butternut squash, cream and olive oil are sure-fire spirit raisers.

When spring seems distant, Butternut Squash, Orange & Ginger makes for a cheerful and refreshing winter lift.

Serves 4

Cooking time: 50 minutes

4 tablespoons olive oil

1 large onion, finely sliced

1 clove garlic, crushed

1 medium butternut squash, peeled and roughly chopped

¼ teaspoon ground ginger

565 ml (1 pint) vegetable stock

100 ml (3½ fl. oz) orange juice

6 tablespoons single cream

Salt and freshly ground black pepper

- Heat the oil in a pan, add the onion and garlic, then cook until soft, without colouring.
- Add the butternut squash and ginger, then cook gently for a further 5 minutes.
- Add the stock and orange juice, bring to the boil, then cover and simmer for 25–30 minutes until the butternut squash is tender.
- Blend until smooth.
- Return to the pan, add the cream, then season to taste. Reheat gently for 5 minutes and serve.

Spinach, Stilton & White Wine

Our connection with Stilton is more than culinary: the village from which the cheese gets its name is only a few miles away from our home at Westwood Farm.

Here, we've teamed Stilton with lightly cooked spinach and a glass of white wine. It's a winter revelation, this soup – masses of swirling green colour and plenty of rich and creamy flavour.

Holding back the spinach till the last moment is the key. That's what gives you the contrast between the smooth and tangy base and the just-wilted bite of green vegetable.

Cooking time: 40 minutes

Serves 4

50 g (2 oz) butter
1 small onion, finely chopped
1 leek, finely chopped
2 sticks celery, finely chopped
2 tablespoons plain flour
5 tablespoons white wine
500 ml (18 fl. oz) vegetable stock
250 g (9 oz) Stilton cheese, crumbled
50 g (2 oz) spinach, washed and chopped
125 ml (¼ pint) milk
2 tablespoons single cream
Salt and freshly ground black pepper

- Melt the butter in a pan, add the onion, leek and celery, then cover and cook for 10 minutes, without colouring.
- Add the flour and cook for 1 minute. Stir in the white wine to make a sauce, then add the stock, bring to the boil, cover and simmer gently for 25 minutes.
- Remove the soup from the heat and add two-thirds of the Stilton, stirring until melted.
- Blend until smooth.
- Place the spinach in a pan with 1 cm/½ inch of boiling water, cover and steam for 3 minutes until tender, then drain well.
- Return the blended soup to the pan, add the milk, season to taste and heat gently for 3 minutes.
- Add the cooked spinach and cream, then serve.

Heart-Warming Chicken Broth

Our sales director, Mike Cassidy, has fond memories of his mother's chicken broth. It seemed like a cure for everything. The soup's magic worked on his daughter, too. Once, when she was three, he had to carry her through 98°F Mediterranean heat in search of a bowl of what she called 'Grandma's chicken broth'. After an hour, he found some chicken soup in a backstreet café.

Here's that miracle-working soup. The method is straightforward; the flavour comes from superb ingredients and long, slow cooking.

Serves 4
Cooking time: 1 hour 30 minutes

4 medium potatoes, diced

2 medium carrots, diced

½ swede, diced

1 medium onion, finely chopped

2 chicken breasts, cut into slices

845 ml (1½ pints) chicken stock

75 g / 3 oz pearl barley

Salt and freshly ground black pepper

- Cook the potatoes in a pan of water for 10 minutes, drain and keep to one side.
- In a new pan add the carrots, swede, onion, chicken, stock and pearl barley.
- Bring to boil and simmer for 15 minutes.
- Add the cooked potatoes, season to taste, then cook for a further 20 minutes and serve.

Creamy Baked Garlic & Onion

Thank goodness onions and garlic are in season all year round. That means we can make this sublime soup any time of the year. Even the preparation is a pleasure. As the slow roasting progresses, your kitchen – perhaps your entire house – fills with the delicious aroma of caramelized garlic and onion.

Slow roasting is the secret to this recipe. After that it's a simple matter of blending to a smooth purée, adding cream, stock and seasonings – and holding back the rush to the table.

Our tip for friendship: don't make this festival of garlic and onion unless everyone eats at least one spoonful.

Serves 4

Cooking time: 2 hours

3 large onions, cut into ½ inch slices

1 bulb garlic, cloves separated and peeled

565 ml (1 pint) chicken stock

1 teaspoon dried thyme

25 g (1 oz) butter

220 ml (8 fl. oz) double cream

1 tablespoon fresh parsley, chopped

Salt and freshly ground black pepper

- Preheat oven to 180°C/gas mark 4.
- Place the onions and garlic in a roasting tin, add 425 ml (¾ pint) of the chicken stock, sprinkle with thyme, season and dot with the butter.
- Cover tightly with foil and bake for 1½ hours. Stirring once or twice during cooking.
- Remove the roasting tin from the oven, cool slightly, then add the remaining stock.
- Blend until smooth.
- Return to the pan, add the cream and parsley, then season to taste. Heat gently for 5 minutes and serve.

Russian Beef Borsch

This borsch comes from Russia with love. According to Mark Billingham (the man who gets our soups on the supermarket shelves, fresh and on time), it's not merely the best borscht he's ever tasted: it's the best soup ever.

Not that Mark is biased. The recipe came from his girlfriend, Margarita. She lives in the Urals and he sees her half a dozen times each year. Absence, as they say, makes the soup lover's heart (and palate) grow fonder. But Mark has a point. There's enough flavour-packed goodness in this chunky beef and beetroot soup to explain why his waistline looks so much fuller after his Russian trips.

Serves 4
Cooking time: 2 hours

250 g (9 oz) raw beetroot, or cooked in natural juices
500 g (1 lb 2 oz) braising steak, cut into 2 cm cubes
1 litre (1¾ pints) beef stock
1 tablespoon olive oil
1 green pepper, diced
2 medium carrots, diced
2 cloves garlic, sliced
1 large onion, chopped
2 medium potatoes, diced
200 g (7 oz) tin chopped tomatoes
200 g (7 oz) shredded red cabbage
2 teaspoons lemon juice
2 teaspoons brown sugar
2 tablespoons fresh dill, chopped
2 tablespoons fresh parsley, chopped
Salt and freshly ground black pepper

- If you have bought raw beetroot wash, trim, wrap in foil and bake for 30–40 minutes at 200°C/gas mark 6 until tender. Cool. Cut cooked beetroot into large dice.
- Place the beef and stock in a pan, bring to boil, then cover and simmer gently for 1 hour and 15 minutes.
- Heat the oil in a separate pan and gently fry the pepper, carrots, garlic and onion for 20 minutes until softened, add to the beef and stock pan.
- Add the potatoes, tomatoes and cabbage to the pan and cook for a further 20 minutes.
- Add the cooked beetroot, lemon juice, sugar and herbs, then season to taste. Cook for a further 5 minutes.
- Remove from the heat, leave to stand for 3 minutes and serve.

Simply Swede

It doesn't take much to bring swede to life. Honey, cream and fresh thyme do the job perfectly well. And, if memories of bland school dinners put you off swede, this is the sweet and creamy soup that will change your opinion.

Look for yellow swedes to add a golden finish to your soup. Vegetable colours tend to fade during cooking, whereas the colour of swede intensifies. Of course, you could grow your own. The six-month gap between sowing and harvest is worth the wait. Lift them before they grow too big, or they'll become woody and unpalatable.

When your soup's ready, finish with a swirl of cream.

Serves 4   Cooking time: 1 hour 20 minutes

1 swede, diced

1 tablespoon honey

3 tablespoons olive oil

Salt & freshly ground black pepper

1 small onion, diced

1 teaspoon thyme, chopped

5 tablespoons double cream

715 ml (1¼ pints) chicken stock

1 teaspoon toasted pumpkin oil

- Preheat the oven to 160°C/gas mark 3.
- Tumble the swede in the honey, 2 tablespoons of olive oil, salt and pepper, then roast in the oven for 1 hour.
- Heat the remaining olive oil in a pan, add the onion and thyme, then cook for 5 minutes until soft with colour.
- Add the roasted swede, cream and chicken stock and bring to the boil.
- Blend until smooth.
- Return to the pan, season to taste, then add the pumpkin oil and serve.

Love & Hearts

Is it still true that the way to a man's heart is through his stomach? Our inventive chef, Amanda Butterfield, wasn't about to take any chances. She planned this passion-provoking Valentine's starter of pancetta, artichoke hearts, wine and cream for her boyfriend, Dan.

History doesn't record whether the ardent couple ever reached the second course of that meal. What we do know is that Dan found Amanda's smooth soups and imaginative flavours irresistible. The pair are now happily married and sipping Love & Hearts from a single shared spoon whenever the mood takes them.

Serves 4

Cooking time: 45 minutes

1 small onion, diced
1 stick celery, diced
1 medium potato, diced
160 g (5½ oz) cannellini beans
25 g (1 oz) pancetta
550 ml (1 pint) water
1 x 400 g (13 oz) tin artichoke hearts, quartered
1 tablespoon white wine
Small bunch parsley, chopped
Pinch ground turmeric
5 tablespoons double cream
Salt and freshly ground black pepper

- Place the onion, celery, potato, cannellini beans, pancetta and water in a pan and bring to the boil. Cover and cook for 20 minutes until the vegetables are soft.
- Blend until smooth.
- Return to the pan, add the artichoke hearts, white wine and parsley, then cook gently for a further 10 minutes.
- Add the turmeric and cream, then season to taste, bring back to the boil and serve.

Spring

March, April & May

Spring

With new growth come new opportunities – tender asparagus, fresh watercress and crisp spring greens. From the seas and rivers come crab, lobster and wild salmon. There are wood pigeons and morel mushrooms in the countryside, and lamb and venison at the farmers' markets. And everywhere else there's enough cheese, chilli, garlic and dried beans to turn the spring harvest into soups suited for a season of hot, cold and in-between weather.

Spring is the time to experiment. Each week brings a wider choice of ingredients; each day seems brighter than the one that went before. Adapt and develop. Choose lettuce, peas and new potatoes for lunching in a sheltered corner of the patio; bring back the cream and squashes to pack a flask for a blustery day on the heath. Make the most of a changeable season.

Roasted Parsnip, Lemon & Vanilla

You don't often find vanilla in a soup. But here it's absolutely right. This is a sweet, smooth, lemon-tinged soup that calls out for something aromatic. We intensified the flavour of the parsnips by roasting, then added a fresh, citrus tang with a sprinkling of lemon zest.

The vanilla pulls it all together to create an intriguing dinner-party dish or a gentle bowl of comfort. It suits just about any occasion you can think of. Serve with parsnip crisps for a burst of crunchy texture.

Serves 4
Cooking time: 45 minutes

- 6 parsnips, roughly diced
- 2 tablespoons olive oil
- 1 small onion, finely chopped
- 1 lemon, zest of
- 1/4 vanilla pod, seeds removed
- 625 ml (22 fl. oz) vegetable stock
- 185 ml (6 1/2 fl. oz) milk
- Salt and freshly ground black pepper

- Preheat oven to 190°C/gas mark 5.
- Roast the parsnips in half the olive oil for 20 minutes until softened and coloured.
- Heat the remaining olive oil in a pan, add the onion and gently cook for 10 minutes until softened.
- Add the lemon zest, vanilla pod and stock and bring to the boil.
- Add the roasted parsnips, cover and simmer gently for 15 minutes.
- Blend until smooth.
- Return to the pan, add the milk, then season to taste. Reheat gently and serve.

Simple Butternut Squash

Jane Parrott, the wife of our marketing director, Nigel, is super-efficient. She has a dozen projects on the go at once, yet she still finds time to boost the kids' vegetable intake. We couldn't understand it, until she gave us her recipe for Simple Butternut Squash.

This is easy, sweet, smooth, creamy and appealing – verging on irresistible. And now we know her secret!

Serves 4

Cooking time: 40 minutes

50 g (2 oz) butter

2 medium onions, finely sliced

3 cloves garlic, sliced

1 large butternut squash, roughly chopped

1 litre (1³/4 pints) water

125 ml (¼ pint) single cream

Salt and freshly ground black pepper

- Melt the butter in a pan and add the onions, garlic and butternut squash.
- Sweat the vegetables for 10 minutes until softened without colouring.
- Add the water, bring to the boil, cover and simmer for 15–20 minutes until soft.
- Blend until smooth.
- Return to the pan and stir in the cream. Season to taste and serve.

Venison Sausage Cassoulet

The rich cassoulets of the Languedoc inspired our operations director, Jim Watson, to put this soup together. His choice of strong venison sausage, meaty haricot beans, bacon and a spoonful of goose fat (or olive oil if you prefer) suggest a meal rather than a snack. He claims that, after a day of heavy digging in the garden, Venison Sausage Cassoulet is the soup that makes it all worthwhile.

Jim's French influences are reinforced by the herbs – bay leaf, thyme, rosemary – that cut through the meaty flavours. This is a soup to bring out the peasant farmer within anyone who's ever sown a few rows of spring seeds.

Serve with crusty French bread.

Serves 4 — Cooking time: 1 hour 15 minutes

1 tablespoon goose fat or olive oil
4 venison sausages
100 g (3½ oz) bacon lardons
2 cloves garlic, crushed
1 small onion, finely diced
1 stick celery, finely chopped
200 g (7 oz) tin tomatoes
1 bay leaf
½ teaspoon fresh thyme, chopped
½ teaspoon fresh rosemary, chopped
500 ml (18 fl. oz) beef stock
410 g (13 oz) tin haricot beans
1 tablespoon tomato purée
Salt and freshly ground black pepper
1 tablespoon fresh parsley, chopped

- Heat the goose fat or olive oil in a pan, add the sausages and fry for 10 minutes, turning frequently until browned, remove from the pan and set aside.
- Add the lardons to the pan and fry until browned; add a little oil if required.
- Add the garlic, onion and celery and cook gently for 5 minutes.
- Add the tomatoes, bay leaf, thyme, rosemary and stock to the pan, then bring to the boil.
- Cut each sausage into 5 and add to the pan. Add the haricot beans, then simmer gently for 30–40 minutes, stirring occasionally, until all the flavours have infused.
- Add the tomato purée, season to taste, then reheat gently for 5 minutes, stirring occasionally.
- Scatter with parsley and serve.

Spinach, Parsley & Honey

A craving for spinach overtook our PR person, Corinna Wilson, when she was pregnant. With time on her hands during maternity leave, she explored new ways to serve what one twelfth-century Arabic writer described as the prince of vegetables.

This bitter-sweet recipe seemed to do the trick. The honey satisfied her sweet tooth, the nip of Worcestershire sauce added piquancy, while the herbs and vegetables kept her fighting fit. She chose baby spinach because, well, that's what motherhood's all about.

Serve with herbed croutons and a motherly hug.

Serves 4

Cooking time: 40 minutes

465 ml (³⁄₄ pint) vegetable stock
1 large carrot, finely chopped or grated
2 sticks celery, chopped
1 small onion, finely diced
285 g (10½ oz) baby spinach
1 tablespoon parsley, chopped
1 tablespoon chives, chopped
4 basil leaves
1 tablespoon honey
180 ml (7 fl. oz) tomato passata
Worcestershire sauce, to taste
Salt and freshly ground black pepper

- Place the stock in a pan and bring to the boil. Add the carrot, celery and onion, then cover and simmer for 15 minutes.
- Add the spinach, herbs, honey and passata, stir and simmer rapidly for 5 minutes.
- Blend, leaving some texture.
- Return to the pan, add the Worcestershire sauce and seasoning to taste. Reheat gently for 2–3 minutes and serve.

Wild Salmon Chowder

The firm and meaty flesh of wild salmon makes for a chunky chowder and a great party dish. When he wants to impress, our operations manager, Alex Faulkner, chooses wild salmon over farmed any day. Here, he's teamed it with a few slivers of smoked salmon for a deeper and smokier flavour.

For an inviting base, Alex says you should grab the first of the year's new potatoes and be generous with the cream and herbs. The result is rich and filling – a little really does go a long way.

Serves 4

Cooking time: 45 minutes

- 25 g (1 oz) butter
- 1 small onion, finely chopped
- 500 g (1 lb 2 oz) new potatoes, halved
- 600 ml (21 fl. oz) fish stock
- 150 g (5 oz) fresh peas
- 550 g (1 lb 3½ oz) wild salmon, cooked
- 2 tablespoons chopped herbs – parsley, mint and chives
- 4 tablespoons double cream
- Salt and freshly ground black pepper
- 100 g (3½ oz) smoked salmon, thin strips

- Melt the butter in a pan, add the onion and cook gently until softened.
- Add the new potatoes and stock, bring to the boil, then cover and simmer gently for 20 minutes until potatoes are tender but intact.
- Remove from the heat, blend half the soup until smooth, return to the pan.
- Add the peas and cook for 2–3 minutes.
- Add the wild salmon, herbs and cream, season to taste and reheat gently.
- Place the smoked salmon strips in the serving bowls, ladle the soup over the top and serve.

Turnip, Honey & Roasted Garlic

Treat a turnip well and it will repay your effort many times over. So here's a soup that takes those tender roots to turnip heaven.

Begin with a long, gentle simmering with carrots and celery to bring out the essential turnip flavour. Towards the end, spoon in the natural sweetness of honey and the fragrant warmth of slow-roasted garlic. Finally, serve with snipped chives for your own heavenly weekend lunch.

Serves 4

Cooking time: 1 hour 15 minutes

25 g (1 oz) butter

1 medium onion, finely diced

3 medium carrots, diced

2 medium potatoes, diced

300 g (10½ oz) turnips, diced

1 stick celery, sliced

750 ml (26 fl. oz) chicken stock

6 cloves garlic – roasted in skin until soft

4 teaspoons honey

Salt and freshly ground black pepper

- Melt the butter in a pan, add the onion and cook gently in a covered saucepan for 10 minutes, without colouring.
- Add the carrots, potatoes, turnips, celery and stock to the pan. Bring to the boil, cover and simmer gently for 1 hour, stirring occasionally.
- Remove from the heat, blend half the soup until smooth and return to the pan.
- Squeeze the roasted garlic cloves from their skins, mash to a paste and add to the soup with the honey. Season to taste, then reheat gently for 2–3 minutes and serve.

Apple, Vine Tomato & Smoked Bacon

On blustery March days, Susie Dobson from our sales team likes to get out on the heath with the family and fly their kites in the wind. Among the discarded gloves, frisbees and half-eaten sweets in her rucksack, she always packs a flask of this sweet and smoky soup.

Susie's Apple, Vine Tomato & Smoked Bacon is a soup that's popular with all age groups. Its appealing orange-red colour, hidden nuggets of crispy bacon and thick, not-quite-smooth texture keep adults warm, kids happy and kites aloft.

Serves 4

Cooking time: 1 hour 30 minutes

25 g (1 oz) butter
1 tablespoon olive oil
1 small onion, finely diced
1 clove garlic, crushed
6 rashers smoked bacon, chopped
600 g (1 lb 5 oz) ripe vine tomatoes, skinned and chopped
2 small Cox's apples, peeled and diced
1 teaspoon brown sugar
500 ml (18 fl. oz) vegetable stock
4–6 fresh sage leaves, very finely sliced
Salt and freshly ground black pepper

- Melt the butter and oil in a pan, add the onion and garlic, then cover and cook gently for 10 minutes, without colouring.
- Add half of the bacon, stirring to stop it sticking for 2 minutes.
- Add the tomatoes, apples, sugar and stock, then bring to the boil. Cover and simmer gently for 1 hour, stirring occasionally.
- Blend until nearly smooth.
- Return the blended soup to the pan, add the sage leaves, season to taste, then reheat gently for 2–3 minutes.
- Meanwhile, fry off the remaining bacon until crispy. Place the crispy bacon into the serving bowls, then ladle the soup over and serve.

Beetroot & Rhubarb

This soup is as sweet, red and appealing as a hand-drawn Mother's Day card. Served with love (how else would you serve soup?), it makes a splendid treat for someone who deserves to put her feet up for a day.

That's what Richard Wilcock (husband of our marketing manager, Helen) thought as Helen's first Mother's Day approached. Once baby Lauren was asleep, he grabbed beetroot and the first of the new-season rhubarb and, in little more than half an hour, turned them into two steaming bowls of affection.

Preparation was child's play, which is why any family can rely on this recipe to give a mother a big red soupy hug.

Serves 4   Cooking time: 35 minutes

25 g (1 oz) butter

300 g (10½ oz) rhubarb, chopped

300 g (10½ oz) cooked beetroot, diced

500 ml (18 fl. oz) vegetable stock

Salt and freshly ground black pepper

- Melt the butter in a pan, add the rhubarb and cook gently until softened.
- Add the beetroot and stock, then bring to the boil. Cover and simmer for 10–15 minutes until the vegetables are tender.
- Blend until smooth.
- Return to the pan, season to taste and serve.

Wood Pigeon & Morel Mushroom

It's lucky for us – and Nigel Parrott (our marketing director) in particular – that the greediest farmland pest makes the most delicious meal. When he was a lad, Nigel used to help protect a neighbouring farmer's spring crops by shooting wood pigeon. By coincidence, spring is when morels – Nigel calls them the king of mushrooms – pop their crinkly heads above ground.

These days Nigel cooks rather than shoots, but he still loves the ingredients he used to gather in his youth. And this is his favourite game soup, simmered with Madeira, red wine and redcurrant jelly. It's as rich and filling as a country-house larder, and as satisfying as if you'd gathered the ingredients yourself.

Serves 4

Cooking time: 40 minutes

1 tablespoon olive oil

2 medium shallots, finely sliced

4 pigeon breasts, sliced

90 g (3¾ oz) morel mushrooms

1 tablespoon red wine vinegar

2 teaspoons redcurrant jelly

100 ml (3½ fl. oz) red wine

2 tablespoons Madeira

550 ml (1 pint) beef stock

Salt & freshly ground black pepper

- Heat the olive oil in a pan, add the shallots, then cook for 5 minutes or until a light golden brown.
- Add the pigeon breasts, cook for 1 minute, then add the morel mushrooms. Cook for a further 2 minutes on a gentle heat.
- Add the red wine vinegar and reduce until it has nearly evaporated. Add the redcurrant jelly, red wine and Madeira, then simmer to reduce by half.
- Add the stock, bring to the boil and cook for 10 minutes. Cover and simmer for 20 minutes.
- Season to taste and serve.

Butternut Squash, Cromer Crab & Chilli

Childhood memories of catching crabs off Cromer pier sparked a lifelong fascination within our marketer, Nick Munby. Since then he's prepared crab in dozens of ways. He says that this recipe always gets dinner-party guests talking.

Nick chose butternut squash for its delicate colour and the ease with which it blends to a smooth base. For the rest, he gives his crab meat an Asian twist with chilli, lemongrass, coriander and coconut milk – cool and spicy flavours that suggest tropical shores far from his starting point on Cromer pier.

Serves 4

Cooking time: 45 minutes

1½ tablespoons olive oil
1 medium onion, finely chopped
1 clove garlic, crushed
1 medium butternut squash, roughly chopped
1 stick lemongrass
1 pinch chilli flakes
500 ml (18 fl. oz) vegetable stock
140 ml (4 ½ fl. oz) coconut milk
120 g (4 ¼ oz) white crab meat, plus brine if using tinned
1 tablespoon fresh coriander, chopped
Salt & freshly ground black pepper
Squeeze of lime

- Heat the olive oil in a pan, add the onion, garlic and butternut squash, then cook gently for 10 minutes.
- Take the stick of lemongrass, remove the tough outer layer and bash with the back of a knife to release the flavours.
- Add the chilli flakes and lemongrass to the pan and fry for 2–3 minutes.
- Add the stock, bring to the boil, then cover and simmer gently for 20 minutes until the squash is tender.
- Cool a little and remove the lemongrass. Blend until smooth.
- Return to the pan, add the coconut milk, crab meat and most of the coriander. Season to taste, then reheat gently for 5 minutes.
- Add a squeeze of lime to taste, sprinkle with the remaining coriander and serve.

Spring Greens

Soups don't get much simpler than this – or much more colourful. This thick and coarse-blended green soup is as bright and cheerful as the first spring greens of the year.

Spring greens are spring cabbages planted close together and picked before the cabbage hearts develop. They're almost as easy to grow as they are to turn into soup. Sow seeds between late July and early August, then transfer seedlings to their final home from late September to early October. If you plant your seedlings about 10cm/4 inches apart and in rows spaced 30 cm/12 inches apart, you can harvest two crops for the same effort. Pick two out of every three cabbages as spring greens, and leave the rest to develop fully.

Serves 4

Cooking time: 40 minutes

200 g (7 oz) spring greens

50 g (2 oz) butter

2 medium potatoes, diced

½ leek, finely sliced

1 onion, finely chopped

500 ml (18 fl. oz) vegetable stock

250 ml (9 fl. oz) milk

Salt and freshly ground black pepper

- Remove the centre stalks from the leaves of the spring greens, shred and wash well.
- Melt the butter in a pan, add the potatoes, leek and onion, then cover and cook for 10 minutes, without colouring, until softened.
- Add the stock, bring to the boil, then cover and simmer for 15 minutes.
- Add the spring greens, cook for a further 3–5 minutes until the greens are tender.
- Blend until the soup has a coarse texture.
- Return to the pan, add the milk, then season to taste. Reheat gently for 3 minutes and serve.

White Onion

Flecks of green parsley and slivers of silvery onion provide the colour and the texture in this creamy, not-quite-white soup. The flavour is as delicate as the colour – sweet and oniony with the lift of white wine.

Serve as a pale and sophisticated starter or as a casual lunchtime treat.
For French onion soups, it seems that white is the new brown.

Serves 4

Cooking time: 1 hour 40 minutes

35 g (1¼ oz) butter

1 tablespoon olive oil

3 medium white onions, finely sliced

1 fat clove garlic, crushed

140 ml (4½ fl. oz) white wine

500 ml (18 fl. oz) chicken stock

140 ml (4½ fl. oz) single cream

1 teaspoon sugar

1 tablespoon fresh parsley, chopped

Salt and freshly ground black pepper

- Melt the butter and olive oil in a pan, add the onions and garlic, then cover and cook over a low heat for 30 minutes without colouring, stirring occasionally.
- The onions should now be nice and soft, with some moisture in the pan from the steam.
- Uncover the pan and continue to cook gently for a further 30 minutes, by which time the onions should be greatly reduced, but still very pale.
- Add the white wine to the pan, then the stock. Cover and simmer for a further 30 minutes.
- Blend half the soup until smooth.
- Return the blended soup to the pan, add the cream, sugar and parsley and season to taste. Heat through for 5 minutes and serve.

Cauliflower & Almond

The luscious cauliflower, cooked till tender and blended till smooth, lies at the heart of many a comforting soup. Its flavour is big enough to stand up for itself, so it won't be bullied into submission by other big-tasting partners.

Here, it stands shoulder to shoulder with almond and nutmeg in an easy, upbeat soup that matches the mood of the season. It's creamy in texture, yet light in tone. In short, this soup is a breeze.

Serves 4

Cooking time: 35 minutes

40 g (1½ oz) ground almonds

1 tablespoon olive oil

1 small onion, finely chopped

1 stick celery, finely chopped

500 ml (18 fl. oz) vegetable stock

1 medium cauliflower, cut into small florets (reserve some for garnish)

140 ml (4½ fl. oz) milk

Salt and freshly ground black pepper

1 pinch grated nutmeg

- In a non-stick frying pan dry-fry the ground almonds over a low to medium heat, stirring constantly until they colour lightly (this helps bring out their flavour). Remove and set to one side.
- Heat the olive oil in the pan, add the onion and celery, then cook gently for 10 minutes until softened.
- Add the stock and ground almonds, then bring to the boil. Add the cauliflower florets (leaving 4 for later) and cook for a further 5 minutes until the cauliflower is just tender.
- Blend until smooth.
- Return to the pan, add the milk, season to taste, then add the remaining cauliflower florets. Reheat gently for 5 minutes until the florets are tender.
- Add the grated nutmeg to taste and serve.

Spicy Turnip & Lentil Dhal

Soups are as healthy, nutritious and inspiring as you want them to be. Fill them with vegetables, lentils and spices, and you've got a meal to see you through the busiest working day.

The dhals of India – there are numerous varieties – are a staple. Our version combines two foods that have been cultivated for thousands of years – protein-rich lentils and tasty turnips – with a colourful range of Eastern spices. The result is a speedy and spicy turnip soup that packs a fiery nutritional punch.

Serves 4

Cooking time: 40 minutes

2 tablespoons olive oil
2 small onions, finely chopped
2 cloves garlic, crushed
1 teaspoon turmeric
½ teaspoon chilli powder
½ teaspoon ground ginger
120 g (4 ¼ oz) red lentils, washed
750 ml (26 fl. oz) water, hot
2 small turnips, finely diced
1 medium carrot, finely diced
3 large tomatoes, skinned and chopped
½ teaspoon garam masala
2 tablespoons coriander, chopped
25 g (1 oz) butter
1½ teaspoons ground cumin

- Heat the olive oil in a pan, add half the onions, then cook for 5 minutes until softened.
- Add the garlic, turmeric, chilli and ginger and fry for 2–3 minutes.
- Add the red lentils and hot water, then bring to the boil. Add the turnips, carrot and tomatoes, cover and simmer for 20 minutes until the vegetables and lentils are tender.
- Add the garam masala and stir well.
- Blend half the soup until smooth.
- Return to the pan with the other unblended soup, reheat gently and stir in the coriander.
- Meanwhile, heat the butter in a pan, add the remaining onions and ground cumin, then cook for 5 minutes until the onions are coloured, sweet and soft.
- Stir the onions and cumin mix into the soup and serve.

Savoy Cabbage & Bacon

Texture can make all the difference to a soup. We often hold back a portion of the ingredients to stir in at the last minute. That simple contrast between smooth and crunchy excites senses that flavours alone can't reach.

Here's a superb example. Shreds of lightly cooked savoy cabbage and crispy bacon swirl through this creamy, pale-green, springtime soup. It tastes as fresh as an April morning, yet it's filling enough for a day at the shops. Serve it when you and your credit card are spent.

Serves 4

Cooking time: 40 minutes

- 300 g (10½ oz) savoy cabbage, shredded
- 25 g (1 oz) butter
- 100 g (3½ oz) dry-cured bacon
- 1 clove garlic, crushed
- 1 small onion, finely chopped
- 1 medium potato, diced
- 600 ml (21 fl. oz) vegetable stock
- 150 ml (5 fl. oz) single cream
- Salt and freshly ground black pepper
- 100 g (3½ oz) bacon lardons

- Select 75 g/3 oz of the shredded cabbage which has a good colour and cook in boiling salted water for 2–3 minutes until *al dente*. Refresh in cold water and keep to one side.
- Melt the butter in a pan, add the dry-cured bacon, followed by the garlic and onion. Cook for 5 minutes without colouring, until softened.
- Add the potato and stock, bring to the boil, then cover and simmer for 10 minutes.
- Add the remaining uncooked cabbage and cook for a further 3–5 minutes until tender but still retains colour.
- Blend until smooth.
- Return to the pan, add the cream and season to taste. Reheat gently for 3 minutes, add the reserved cooked cabbage.
- Meanwhile, fry off the lardons until they are coloured and crispy.
- Place the lardons in the serving bowls, ladle the soup over and serve.

Chocolate & Rhubarb Swirl

Our recipe-development team aren't known for their self-restraint. But once a year they make a collective act of sacrifice and give up chocolate for Lent. It's a tough challenge with a huge prize at the end – their Chocolate & Rhubarb Swirl. Whenever they serve this scrummy dessert soup, everyone scrambles for second helpings. The heavenly taste and unusual two-tone, fruit-and-chocolate ripples are an unmissable Easter treat.

Serves 4
Cooking time: 40 minutes

Rhubarb Soup
300 g (10½ oz) rhubarb, chopped
100 ml (3½ fl. oz) apple & blackberry juice
3 tablespoons clear honey
100 ml (3½ fl. oz) white wine
½ teaspoon cornflour, mixed with a little cold water
1 or 2 drops rosewater (optional)

Chocolate Soup
75 g (3 oz) dark chocolate (70% cocoa solids), broken into small chunks
150 ml (5 fl. oz) milk
150 ml (5 fl. oz) double cream
2 egg yolks
½ teaspoon cornflour, mixed with a little cold water
2 tablespoons golden caster sugar

- To make the rhubarb soup, place the rhubarb, apple & blackberry juice, honey and white wine into a pan. Bring to the boil, then cover and simmer gently for 10 minutes until the fruit is softened.
- Blend until smooth. Return to the pan, add the water and cornflour mix, and stir over a low heat until thickened. Add one or two drops of rosewater to taste and set to one side.
- To make the chocolate soup, place the chocolate, milk and cream in a bowl over a pan of simmering water, stirring until the chocolate has melted.
- In a clean bowl whisk together the egg yolks, cornflour mix and sugar.
- Pour the warmed chocolate milk onto the egg mixture, whisking as you pour. Once they're thoroughly mixed together, return the mixture to the pan.
- Stir continuously over a low heat until the mixture starts to thicken and bubble.
- If not to be eaten immediately, place some cling film over the chocolate soup to prevent a skin forming.
- Pour the chocolate soup into the bowls, ripple with the rhubarb soup and serve.

Lobster Bisque

A bisque is a rich, shellfish soup – usually of lobster. It's exactly the kind of recipe that sends Nikki Fawcett (the one who holds our HQ together) scurrying for a saucepan, the cognac and a guest list.

Nikki cooks lobster as often as she can afford it. And this traditional bisque is about as rich and creamy a lobster recipe as she can find. If she can't get fresh lobster, she'll happily use ready-prepared. She's also relaxed about her choice of spirits – either brandy or calvados will do.

The main thing is that the dish should be fun – creamy and fishy in equal measure and chock-full of lobster.

Serves 4

Cooking time: 45 minutes

1 small lobster, fresh & whole

40 g (1½ oz) unsalted butter

1 medium onion, sliced

30 g (1¼ oz) plain flour

1 tablespoon tomato purée

2 tablespoons brandy or calvados

600 ml (21 fl. oz) fish stock

75 ml (3 fl. oz) double cream

Salt & freshly ground black pepper

1 teaspoon parsley, chopped

- Take the lobster and place in a pan of cold water. Heat gently for 30 minutes, until the lobster is light pink in colour; do not allow to boil. Remove from the heat and allow to cool in the water.
- Once cool, remove the lobster from the water and place on a chopping board. Remove the claws, cut the lobster in half lengthways and remove the meat, taking care to avoid any discoloured meat (green, brown or black).
- Whilst the lobster is cooking, melt the butter in a pan, add the onion and cook until soft without any colour.
- Add the flour and stir well, then add the tomato purée, stir in well and cook for 30 seconds.
- Add the brandy or calvados and reduce the volume by half. Add the fish stock and keep stirring until the soup comes to the boil and starts to thicken. Cover and simmer gently for 25 minutes.
- Blend until smooth.
- Return to the pan, add the lobster meat and double cream, then season to taste.
- Bring back to a simmer for 3 minutes, sprinkle over the parsley and serve.

Broad Bean & Bacon

Our brand manager, Dan Gough, leads a comfortable, well-fed existence. His fiancée, Heidi, loves the kitchen, cook books and food magazines; he loves to eat whatever she cooks.

Every so often, Dan brings in one of Heidi's recipes (presumably in the hope that we might make it, too). In this case he struck gold: Heidi cooked Broad Bean & Bacon at home and we cooked Broad Bean & Bacon at work. It's that kind of recipe.

Serves 4

Cooking time: 35 minutes

1 tablespoon olive oil

12 rashers of smoked, streaky bacon, cut into strips

12 spring onions, roughly chopped

750 ml (26 fl. oz) vegetable stock

500 g (1 lb 2 oz) broad beans

Salt and freshly ground black pepper

- Heat the olive oil in a pan, add the bacon and spring onions, then cook for 8–10 minutes until the bacon starts to crisp.
- Add some of the stock to the pan and cook gently for a further 3 minutes.
- Add the broad beans and the remaining stock, then cook for 20 minutes.
- Blend until smooth.
- Return to the pan, season to taste and serve.

Petits Pois & Watercress

This is just about the quickest soup of the year. It's light and refreshing, too, which makes it the perfect snack for the first sunny days on the patio. You can prepare it when the skies look promising and, chances are, you'll have your bowls in the dishwasher long before the clouds return.

Nothing in this soup needs much cooking. Watercress and the sweet petits pois of spring blend to a smooth green purée after a couple of minutes in the pan. After that, all you need is a sprinkling of fresh mint.

Serves 4

Cooking time: 20 minutes

25 g (1 oz) butter

1 medium onion, finely chopped

350 g (12 oz) fresh peas

50 g (2 oz) watercress

750 ml (26 fl. oz) vegetable stock

Salt & freshly ground black pepper

1½ tablespoons fresh mint, chopped

- Melt the butter in a pan, add the onion, then cook for 5 minutes until soft.
- Add the peas, watercress and stock, then bring to boil. Cover and simmer for 5 minutes until the peas are tender.
- Blend until smooth.
- Return to the pan, season to taste and reheat gently for 3 minutes. Add the chopped mint and serve.

Hungarian Lamb

Memories of a grey day in Budapest inspired Hannah, the wife of our Colin Wilson (he keeps our soup deliveries flowing), to make this soup. It wasn't so much the weather as the vibrant colours of the street stalls and the tempting smell of home cooking from nearby cafés that captured Hannah's imagination. The city was alive with spicy red food.

Hannah absorbed it all and, on her return to England, bought lamb, pepper and paprika. Now anyone can turn grey into red with Hannah's chunky, stewlike soup.

Serves 4
Cooking time: 1 hour 15 minutes

1 tablespoon olive oil
175 g (6 oz) lamb fillet, cut into cubes
1 medium onion, finely chopped
1 clove garlic, crushed
600 ml (21 fl. oz) lamb stock
200 g (7 oz) tin chopped tomatoes
½ teaspoon smoked paprika
1 bay leaf
½ teaspoon caraway seeds, lightly crushed
1 small stick celery, chopped
1 small carrot, diced
1 small potato, diced
75 g (3 oz) swede, diced
½ red pepper, diced
1 heaped tablespoon mini pasta
1 tablespoon tomato purée
1 tablespoon fresh parsley, chopped
Salt & freshly ground black pepper

- Heat the olive oil in a pan, add the lamb, onion and garlic, then fry until the meat is browned and the onion golden brown.
- Add the stock, tomatoes, paprika, bay leaf and caraway seeds, stir and bring to boil. Cover and simmer gently for 30 minutes.
- Add the vegetables and mini pasta, cover and simmer for a further 20–30 minutes until vegetables and pasta are tender.
- Stir in the tomato purée and parsley, then season to taste. Reheat gently for 3 minutes and serve.

Pea, Herb & Lettuce

You probably remember those childhood tales in which rabbits ate too much lettuce and fell asleep in the sun. That's unlikely to happen with this fresh green pea and lettuce soup, but it does make for a peaceful afternoon lunch or a late-evening snack.

Preparation is stress-free, too. A few minutes' cooking and a quick whizz in the blender is enough to pull this creamy and not-quite-smooth soup together.

Take it slowly, share it with friends, and cancel the rest of the day's appointments.

Serves 4
Cooking time: 20 minutes

25 g (1 oz) butter

300 g (10½ oz) fresh peas

1 small head (150 g / 5 oz) of soft lettuce (e.g. iceberg), torn into pieces

3 small spring onions, finely sliced

2 tablespoons parsley, roughly chopped

2 tablespoons coriander, roughly chopped

650 ml (23 fl. oz) vegetable stock

100 ml (3½ fl. oz) single cream

Salt & freshly ground black pepper

- Melt the butter in a pan, add the peas, lettuce and spring onions. Cook gently until the lettuce has wilted.
- Add the herbs and cook for a further minute. Add the stock and simmer gently, uncovered for 3 minutes.
- Remove from the heat, remove 2 ladlefuls of soup and set to one side in a bowl.
- Blend the remaining soup until smooth.
- Return the blended soup and the soup left to one side to the pan and reheat for 3 minutes.
- Add the cream and season to taste. Heat gently for 2 minutes and serve.

Asparagus, Leek & New Potato Chowder

Soup flows in the blood of the Down family. Ray and his wife, Jan, and brother, Les, all work with us. As you can imagine, soup plays a big part in family gatherings.

This is a chunky spring favourite that they tuck into when soft-skinned new potatoes and tender asparagus come into season. The Down family tip is to leave the skins on the new potatoes. It's not just that the skins are the best bit, but they make the job of getting soup to the table that much quicker – an important consideration when there's a whole tribe to feed.

Serves 4

Cooking time: 30 minutes

25 g (1 oz) butter

1 leek, white part only, finely sliced

250 g (9 oz) new potatoes, halved

500 ml (18 fl. oz) vegetable stock

500 g (1 lb 2 oz) asparagus, trimmed and cut into 2 cm lengths

½ teaspoon finely chopped tarragon

150 ml (5 fl. oz) single cream

1 tablespoon parsley, finely chopped

Salt & freshly ground black pepper

- Melt the butter in a pan, add the leek and cook for 5 minutes until soft.
- Add the potatoes and stock, then bring to the boil. Cover and simmer gently for 15 minutes until the potatoes are almost tender.
- Stir in the asparagus and tarragon, then cook for a further 3–5 minutes until asparagus is *al dente*.
- Remove one-third of the soup and blend until smooth.
- Return the blended soup to the pan, stir in the cream and parsley, then season to taste. Reheat gently for 3 minutes and serve.

Radish, Spring Onion & Lettuce

The cheerful radish, red and peppery, rarely strays beyond the salad bar. It's a shame, because radishes add colour, flavour and a delightfully crisp texture. In contrast, those flirtatious salad ingredients, lettuce and spring onion, often find their way into soups and stews.

So here's a compromise: all three salad ingredients together in one healthy soup that shouts 'springtime'. And, just to make sure they get on fine, we've set them in a base of peas, potato and double cream.

If that sounds like a bowlful of late-spring comfort, you'd be right.

Serves 4
Cooking time: 45 minutes

- 25 g (1 oz) unsalted butter
- 1 medium potato, diced
- 1 small onion, diced
- 75 g (3 oz) peas
- 520 ml (18 fl. oz) vegetable stock
- 100 g (3½ oz) lettuce, leaves removed and washed
- 3 spring onions, sliced
- 4 radishes, sliced
- Salt & freshly ground black pepper
- 3 tablespoons double cream
- 1 teaspoon parsley, chopped

- Melt the butter in a pan, add the potato and onion, then cook for 3 minutes until soft.
- Add the peas and vegetable stock, bring to the boil, then cover and simmer for 25 minutes.
- Remove the lid and add the lettuce, cook for a further 5 minutes.
- Blend until smooth.
- Return to the pan, add the spring onions and radishes, then season to taste.
- Cook gently for 5 minutes, then add the cream and chopped parsley. Stir and serve.

Sweet Potato & Spring Fruits

Here's a dinner-party dish that bubbles with inventiveness. It's fiery, fruity, zesty and sweet – and easily adapted to suit your tastes.

To produce the intense depth of flavour, you build it up, layer by layer, on a smooth base of sweet potato. There's the heat and spice of spring onion, chilli and coriander; the tang of lemon and lime; the fruitiness of apricot and rhubarb; and, finally, the crispness of white wine. Finish with chunks of sweet potato and torn basil leaves.

Serves 4
Cooking time: 3 hours

25 g (1 oz) butter
1 tablespoon olive oil
2 sweet potatoes, large cubes
2 spring onions, chopped
½ small green chilli, finely chopped
½ teaspoon ground coriander
½ lemon, zest of
½ lime, zest of
200 g (7 oz) rhubarb, chopped
100 g (3½ oz) ready-to-eat apricots, chopped
1 teaspoon brown sugar
100 ml (3½ fl. oz) dry white wine
650 ml (23 fl. oz) vegetable stock
4 basil leaves, torn
Salt & freshly ground black pepper

- Heat the butter and oil in a pan, add the sweet potatoes, then cook gently until lightly coloured.
- Add the spring onions, chilli, coriander, lemon and lime zests and cook for a further 3–4 minutes.
- Add the rhubarb, apricots, sugar, wine and stock, then bring to boil. Cover and simmer for 15 minutes or until tender.
- Carefully remove 12 chunks of sweet potato from the soup and put to one side.
- Blend the rest of the soup until smooth.
- Return to the pan and reheat gently. Add the chunks of sweet potato and torn basil leaves, season to taste and serve.

Summer

June, July & August

Summer

When the sun is high and the shade is cool, a chilled summer soup is all the refreshment you need. These are the carefree months when soups are as easy as your mood and as relaxed as your guests.

At this time of year, no two soups need ever be the same. There are just too many ingredients to choose from. Greenhouses swell with tomatoes and cucumbers; allotments are heavy with peas and beans; while soft fruit ripens as fast as you can pick it.

For grander soups, there's tender lamb and the first of the grouse, while fish and seafood reflect our eternal love affair with the sea and outdoor eating.

Summer is for soups packed with life and fragrant, hand-picked garden herbs; summer is for cooking quickly, eating light and digesting slowly.

Asparagus, Cucumber & Pea

You know summer's arrived when you can drop fresh asparagus, cucumber and pea into the same saucepan. It's worth inviting your friends round to celebrate.

They won't be disappointed. With so many fresh, summery herbs and vegetables in their bowls, they'll feel as excited as you are. When they discover the delicate tips of asparagus that you added at the last minute, they'll count it as a bonus.

Serves 4

Cooking time: 25 minutes

250 g (9 oz) asparagus, chopped (but reserve tips)
50 g (2 oz) butter
1 medium onion, finely chopped
250 g (9 oz) leeks, finely sliced
1 clove garlic, finely chopped
¼ cucumber, diced
125 g (4½ oz) fresh peas, shelled
750 ml (26 fl. oz) vegetable stock
3 tablespoons chives, snipped
1 tablespoon of each chopped: parsley, thyme, rosemary, coriander
½ tablespoon sage leaves, chopped
½ tablespoon mint leaves, chopped
Salt & freshly ground black pepper

- Place the asparagus tips in a little water and steam for 3 minutes until *al dente*, refresh in cold water and leave to one side.
- Melt the butter in a pan, then cook the onion, leeks and garlic for 5 minutes, without colouring.
- Add the chopped asparagus, cucumber and peas, stir to coat with the butter, then cook for 2 minutes.
- Add the stock, rapidly bring to the boil, then cover and simmer for 5–7 minutes until vegetables are just tender but retain their colour.
- Blend until smooth.
- Return to the pan, add the chopped herbs and asparagus tips, then season to taste. Reheat gently for 2 minutes and serve.

Smoked Mackerel & Horseradish

This two-part soup is both filling and playful. Everyone loves to swirl the complementary colours, flavours and textures together and to savour the varying tastes – tangy from the horseradish, then smoky with the fish.

We serve it with crusty bread on long summer evenings when the sun never seems to set. After we've stirred and dipped our soup, we scrape the bowls clean, then sit back to watch the colours drain from the evening skies.

Serves 4

Cooking time: 40 minutes

50 g (2 oz) butter
1 medium onion, finely chopped
1 clove garlic, crushed
2 medium potatoes, diced
750 ml (26 fl. oz) water
280 g (10 oz) smoked mackerel, skin removed and flaked
1 tomato, peeled, deseeded and chopped
1 teaspoon lemon juice
1 tablespoon fresh parsley, chopped
1 tablespoon fresh chives, chopped
Salt & freshly ground black pepper
3 tablespoons double cream
3 tablespoons hot horseradish sauce

- **Melt the butter in a pan, add the onion, garlic and potatoes, then cook gently for 10 minutes until softened.**
- **Add the water, bring to the boil, then cover and simmer for 15 minutes until the potatoes are tender. Add two-thirds of the mackerel.**
- **Blend until smooth.**
- **Return to the pan, heat gently, then add the remaining mackerel, tomato, lemon juice and herbs, reserving a few for garnish. Season to taste.**
- **Mix the cream, horseradish and remaining herbs together, ladle the soup into the serving bowls, then finish with a spoonful of the herby horseradish cream.**

Baby Vegetable & Minted Lamb Broth

Three generations of Anne Jackson's family have relied on this lamb broth to provide many years of lazy Sunday lunches in the garden. Anne (wife of Martin Jackson, another one of our PR gurus) says that the key to the flavour lies in the marinating of the lamb. The longer you leave it, the deeper the flavour. After that, everything comes together in less than half an hour – which means cooks can enjoy the sunshine as much as everyone else.

Cooking time: 20 minutes

Serves 4

- 1 tablespoon fresh parsley, chopped
- 1 tablespoon olive oil
- 1 clove garlic, crushed
- 200 g (7 oz) lamb fillet
- Salt & freshly ground black pepper
- 1 litre (1¾ pints) vegetable stock
- 100 g (3½ oz) baby carrots, cut into batons
- 100 g (3½ oz) fresh peas
- 100 g (3½ oz) broad beans, shelled (weight is pre-shelled)
- Pinch sugar
- 2 tablespoons fresh mint, chopped
- 1 tablespoon chives, chopped
- 5–6 radishes, cut into small wedges
- 4 spring onions, finely sliced

- Mix the parsley, olive oil and garlic together, then spoon over the lamb fillet, leave to marinate for at least 30 minutes, preferably 2 hours, in the fridge.
- Remove the marinated lamb from the fridge and bring to room temperature 30 minutes before cooking.
- Heat a pan, season the lamb and place in the hot pan. Cook for 3–4 minutes on each side. This will leave your lamb pink in the middle; cook for longer if required. Remove the lamb from the pan, cover with foil and leave to one side.
- Place the vegetable stock in the pan and bring to the boil, add the carrots, then cover and boil for 2 minutes.
- Add the peas and broad beans, then cook for a further 3–5 minutes. At this stage the vegetables should be *al dente*.
- Add the sugar, most of the herbs, radishes and spring onions, then season to taste. Cook for a further 3 minutes on a gentle heat.
- Finely slice the lamb across the fillet – you should aim for 5–7 slices per portion.
- Place the sliced lamb into the serving bowls, ladle the soup over the top, then sprinkle with the remaining herbs and serve.

Broad Bean, Feta Cheese & Smoked Salmon

A shady spot and a bowl of refreshing soup are as much as anyone needs for a quick break from a day on the go. This is a dish of summer surprises, filled with smooth broad bean, hidden strips of smoked salmon and melted feta.

This is the soup for upbeat days when you want to knock the garden into shape rather than fall asleep in it. It's fun, lively and – dare we say it? – full of beans.

Serves 4

Cooking time: 30 minutes

25 g (1 oz) butter

1 medium onion, finely chopped

1 medium potato, finely diced

500 g (1 lb 2 oz) broad beans

1 tablespoon young thyme, chopped

750 ml (26 fl. oz) vegetable stock

Salt & freshly ground black pepper

1½ tablespoons fresh parsley

100 g (3½ oz) feta cheese, crumbled

100 g (3½ oz) smoked salmon, fine strips

- Melt the butter in a pan, add the onion and potato, then cover and cook for 10 minutes without colouring until soft.
- Add the broad beans, thyme and stock and bring to boil. Cover and simmer for 5–10 minutes until vegetables are tender but not overcooked.
- Blend until smooth.
- Return to the pan, season to t , then reheat gently for 2 minutes. Add the chopped parsley.
- Crumble the feta into the centre of the serving bowls and top with the smoked-salmon strips, ladle the soup over the top and serve.

"Golden Silk" Carrot, Mango & Cumin

Our PR specialist Alison Saunders' fondness for southern France – and for its cooking – is deep-rooted. The endless sunshine and colourful produce draw her back to St-Tropez year after year.

This is the soup that she says captures the lazy warmth of the French Mediterranean. Alison calls it Golden Silk because that's what it looks and tastes like. Her soup is rich, smooth and fruity with a piquant nip of spices and sherry. The finishing touch is a sprinkling of croutons.

Serves 4

Cooking time: 1 hour 20 minutes

- 50 g (2 oz) butter
- 2 medium onions, finely sliced
- 1 teaspoon turmeric
- ½ teaspoon fresh ground nutmeg
- ½ teaspoon ground coriander
- ½ teaspoon ground cumin
- 450 g (1 lb) young carrots, sliced
- 150 g (5 oz) ripe mango, chopped
- 150 ml (5 fl. oz) dry sherry
- 800 ml (28 fl. oz) water
- 4 tablespoons double cream
- Salt & freshly ground black pepper

- Melt the butter in a pan, add the onions, then cook gently without colouring for 10 minutes until softened.
- Add the spices and cook for a further 2 minutes.
- Add the carrots, mango and sherry, then cook gently for a further 5 minutes without colouring.
- Add the water, bring to the boil, then cover and simmer over a gentle heat for 45 minutes to 1 hour.
- Blend until smooth.
- Return to the pan, add the cream, then reheat gently for 3 minutes. Season to taste and serve.

Summer Sorrel, Swiss Chard & Lemon Thyme

Grab bitter, spear-shaped sorrel leaves when you can, and cook them quick before they wilt. But that's what this fresh and zesty soup is all about – sharp flavours at their seasonal best.

This is a grown-up dish for a sultry summer dinner party. The flavours of sorrel, chard (a close relative of beetroot), lemon thyme, sherry and shallot linger on the palate, while the creamy finish puts you in the mood for a night of midsummer magic.

Serves 4

Cooking time: 30 minutes

50 g (2 oz) butter
3 shallots, finely chopped
150 g (5 oz) sorrel leaves
250 g (9 oz) Swiss chard, stalks removed, chopped
1 tablespoon lemon thyme
1 lemon, zest and juice of
1 dessertspoon dry sherry
250 ml (9 fl. oz) milk
½ teaspoon brown sugar
500 ml (18 fl. oz) chicken stock
1½ teaspoons cornflour, mixed with a little cold water
Salt & freshly ground black pepper
4 tablespoons double cream

- Melt the butter in a pan, add the shallots, then cook gently for 5–10 minutes until softened, without colouring.
- Add the sorrel, Swiss chard, lemon thyme and lemon zest. Stir to wilt the leaves.
- Add the sherry, milk, lemon juice, sugar and stock, then bring to the boil quickly and simmer for 2–3 minutes.
- Blend until smooth.
- Return to the pan, then reheat gently for 2 minutes. Add the cornflour and cook until thickened slightly. Season to taste, then finish with the cream and serve.

Watercress & New Potato

Our chief foodie, Mike Faers submitted this recipe to our book for its credentials as a summer classic from his days as a Le Gavroche chef. Mike is a firm believer that making good soup is all about using great seasonal ingredients and cooking them with respect. Always one to share his vision and inventiveness with the rest of the team, this soup is definitely worth a try - what Mike doesn't know about soups and soup making isn't worth knowing! Serve this soup to your friends as a light treat and wow them with a restaurant-worthy dish evoking the traditional flavours of summer.

Cooking time: 30 minutes

Serves 4

- 25 g (1 oz) butter
- 1 medium onion, finely sliced
- 1 clove garlic, crushed
- 250 g (9 oz) new salad potatoes, halved
- 800 ml (28 fl. oz) vegetable stock
- 400 g (13 oz) watercress, hard stalks removed
- 3 tablespoons double cream
- Salt & freshly ground black pepper
- ½ lemon, juice of
- ½ teaspoon freshly grated nutmeg

- Melt the butter in a pan, add the onion, garlic and new potatoes, then cover and cook gently for 10 minutes, without colouring.
- Add the stock, bring to the boil and simmer for 5 minutes.
- Add the watercress, bring to the boil, then cook for 4 minutes, retaining the colour in the watercress.
- Remove from the heat, remove some chunks of potato and leave to one side.
- Blend the rest of the soup until smooth.
- Return to the pan, add the reserved potato chunks and cream, then reheat gently for 3 minutes.
- Season to taste. Add the lemon juice to taste, then add the grated nutmeg and serve.

Summer Berry

We were knocked out when we first tasted this dessert soup. It screams fruit and freshness. Now we can't imagine summer without it.

You don't have to follow our list of fruit. Use whatever you can lay your hands on – whatever's ripening on the day you make it. But don't compromise on the orange zest, white wine and crème de cassis. These are the luxury ingredients that turn Summer Berry into an indulgent lunchtime treat or a stunning after-dinner finale.

Serve warm or cool with toasted flaked almonds and crème fraîche or ice cream.

Serves 4

Cooking time: 1 hour

300 g (10½ oz) rhubarb, cut into lengths
2 apples, peeled and chopped
450 g (1 lb) mixed berries (we use a mix of: raspberries, blueberries, blackcurrants, cherries, blackberries)
300 g (10½ oz) berries to finish (we use 100 g of each: raspberries, cherries, blueberries)
75 g (3 oz) caster sugar
300 ml (10½ fl. oz) white wine
1 orange, zest of
2 tablespoons crème de cassis
Lemon juice or honey

- Preheat the oven to 180°C/gas mark 4.
- In an ovenproof dish, place the rhubarb, apples and 450 g/1 lb mixed berries (reserve the additional 300 g/10½ oz berries to use later). Sprinkle with the sugar and bake for 30–40 minutes until the rhubarb is tender.
- The fruits should be glossy and be sitting in their own juices. Remove from the oven and cool the fruit.
- Blend until smooth, then push through a sieve to remove the pips from the fruit. Leave to one side.
- Heat the wine and orange zest in a pan and slowly bring to the boil to infuse the orange.
- Remove from the heat, discard the orange zest, then add the crème de cassis. Mix with the puréed fruits. Taste the purée, adjust the sweetness by adding lemon juice or honey to taste.
- Add the reserved berries, stir, then serve warm, or allow to cool.

Beautiful Broccoli

A head of broccoli is as beautiful as a bunch of flowers – which is exactly what it is: a tight cluster of flower buds. Broccoli reached Britain via Italy (*broccoli* means 'little shoots') and was originally known as Italian asparagus.

For great soup, packed with vitamins and fibre, choose broccoli with fresh-smelling, compact heads. Check also that the cut stems at the base aren't dry or cracked. And for beautiful green soup, whizz your cooked ingredients until smooth, stir in crème fraîche and serve with Roquefort croutons.

Serves 4
Cooking time: 40 minutes

25 g (1 oz) butter

1 small onion, finely chopped

1 medium potato, diced

170 g (6 oz) broccoli, cut into florets

1 courgette, large chunks

1 celery stick, sliced

540 ml (18½ fl. oz) vegetable stock

Salt and freshly ground black pepper

2 tablespoons crème fraîche

- Melt the butter in a pan, add the onion and potato, then cook gently for 5–10 minutes, without colouring.
- Add the rest of the vegetables and cook gently for a further 2 minutes, without colouring.
- Add the stock, bring to the boil, then cover and simmer for 15–20 minutes until vegetables are tender.
- Blend until smooth.
- Return to the pan and season to taste. Reheat gently for 3 minutes, stir in the crème fraîche and serve.

Broad Bean & Garlic

Removing the skins from blanched broad beans isn't something you want to do every day. But this is July, so you might as well do the job outside in the sunshine. The effort is worth it. Broad Bean & Garlic is much lighter than you expect. It's a warm, garlic-tinged soup bursting with summer herbs.

To make the most of your handywork, serve with shavings of Parmesan and a drizzle of olive oil.

Serves 4

Cooking time: 1 hour

600 g (1 lb 5 oz) broad beans

1 tablespoon olive oil

1 medium onion, finely chopped

2 cloves garlic, crushed

1 tablespoon basil, chopped

1 tablespoon parsley, chopped

1 tablespoon chives, chopped

750 ml (26 fl. oz) chicken stock

Salt and freshly ground black pepper

- Shell the broad beans by blanching them in boiling water for 2–3 minutes, refresh in cold water, then slip the skins off by squeezing each bean gently. This is time-consuming but essential for this soup!
- Heat the olive oil in a pan, add the onion and garlic, then cover and cook gently for 10–15 minutes until softened, without colouring.
- Add the shelled broad beans, herbs and stock, then bring to boil and simmer for 5 minutes.
- Blend half the soup until smooth.
- Return to the pan and season to taste. Reheat for 3 minutes and serve

Crab & Artichoke

Here's a soup for a day of cliff-top walks, beachcombing, rock-pooling and fresh sea air. It's the soup that everyone will tuck into while they argue over who found the smoothest pebble and the largest crab.

The rivalry will soon fade once they have a few spoonfuls of this rich and creamy soup inside them. Serve with chunks of crusty bread and your beachcombers will feel as happy and fulfilled as if they'd discovered pirate treasure.

Serves 4

Cooking time: 40 minutes

- 25 g (1 oz) butter
- ½ small leek, finely sliced
- 1 celery stick, diced
- 2 shallots, finely chopped
- 2 x 400 g (14 oz) tins artichoke hearts (2 x 240 g / 8½ oz drained weight)
- 500 ml (18 fl. oz) vegetable stock
- 1 tablespoon young thyme, chopped
- 150 ml (5 fl. oz) single cream
- 170 g (6 oz) white crabmeat
- 1 tablespoon parsley
- 1 tablespoon lemon juice
- Salt and freshly ground black pepper

- Melt the butter in a pan, add the leek, celery and shallots, then cook gently for 10 minutes, without colouring.
- Add the artichokes, stock and thyme, and bring to the boil. Cover and simmer for 15 minutes.
- Blend two-thirds of the soup until smooth and put to one side.
- Blend the remaining third until it has a coarse and pulpy texture.
- Combine the blended soups in the pan, add the cream, crabmeat, parsley and lemon juice.
- Season to taste, then reheat gently for 5 minutes and serve.

Summer Fruits with Mango Custard

Our Michelle Harriman – the brand manager who keeps us on our toes – has a sweet tooth and a clever way of turning fruits into thick and creamy custards. It's not just an attractive dinner-party dessert: Michelle's toddler Dorothy (Dotty) loves it too.

Follow Michelle's lead and top her lime, coconut and mango custard with a selection of soft summer fruits. Her advice is to serve it cold and use whatever fruits you have to hand. If time is tight or you can't get hold of fresh mangoes, puréed mango will work just as well.

Serves 4

Cooking time: 30 minutes

- 284 ml (½ pint) double cream
- 284 ml (½ pint) coconut milk
- 1 lime, zest of
- 6 egg yolks
- 2 tablespoons caster sugar
- 2 teaspoons cornflour
- 150 g (5 oz) mango, puréed
- 400 g (13 oz) soft fruits (for example, cherries, blueberries, blackberries and raspberries), washed and drained

- Heat the cream, coconut milk and lime zest in a pan until it just comes to the boil.
- Meanwhile, whisk together the egg yolks, sugar and cornflour in a bowl until smooth.
- Pour the hot cream into the egg yolk mixture, whisking all the time.
- Return the mixture to the pan and reheat gently, stirring continuously until it thickens.
- Strain through a sieve into a bowl to remove the lime zest and cool.
- Mix the cooled custard with the mango purée, then ladle into the serving bowls. Top with the soft fruit and serve.

Strawberry, Cream & Champagne

The name of this dessert soup says it all. As soon as you hear it, you start wondering whether there's anything in your wardrobe that's light and floaty enough for a garden party.

The concept seems simple, yet it took someone like our graphic designer, Mark Rylands (the handwriting in this book and on our soup cartons is his), to bring the idea to life. He blended, sieved and thickened his champagne-soaked strawberries to create a smooth red base, then finished with more champagne-soaked strawberries and a generous swirl of thick cream.

If ever there was a designer dessert, this is it.

Serves 4

Cooking time: 30 minutes

1 kg (2 lb 4 oz) ripe strawberries, reserving 200 g (7 oz) for garnish

430 ml (³/4 pint) champagne or sparkling wine

Caster sugar or honey, if required

1½ teaspoons cornflour, mixed with a little water

285 ml (10½ fl. oz) extra-thick single cream

- Wash and hull the strawberries, then cut them into quarters.
- Soak the reserved 200 g/7 oz strawberries in one-third of the champagne for at least 1 hour at room temperature.
- Blend the remaining strawberries until smooth, then sieve into a pan to remove the seeds. Ripe strawberries should be sweet enough but, if they need to be sweeter, add honey or caster sugar to taste.
- Add the remaining champagne to the pan and gently bring to a simmer.
- Add the cornflour, stirring continuously until thickened, then stir in the single cream.
- Serve warm or chilled, decorating with the remaining champagne-soaked strawberries.

Potato, Sorrel & Goat's Cheese

The bitter lemon acidity of sorrel and the creaminess of mild goat's cheese make a great dinner-party pairing. They sound sophisticated, yet the method is straight forward. The magic comes from the blend of flavours and the unexpected chunks of melting goat's cheese and flecks of snipped chives hidden within each bowl.

Serve indoors to set the mood of the party, or outdoors to stave off the chill of a late-summer evening.

Sorrel isn't always easy to come by. Use spinach if you can't find it.

Serves 4
Cooking time: 40 minutes

150 g (5 oz) soft mild goat's cheese

25 g (1 oz) butter

1 medium onion, finely chopped

1 clove garlic, crushed

2 medium potatoes, diced

750 ml (26 fl. oz) chicken stock

225 g (8 oz) sorrel leaves

100 ml (3½ fl. oz) single cream

Salt and freshly ground black pepper

1 tablespoon chives, snipped

- Remove the goat's cheese from the fridge and bring to room temperature.
- Heat the butter in a pan, add the onion, garlic and potatoes, then cook gently for 10 minutes, without colouring.
- Add the stock and bring to the boil. Cover and simmer for 10 minutes until the potatoes are tender.
- Add the sorrel leaves and cook for a further 5 minutes.
- Blend until smooth.
- Return to the pan, add the cream, then season to taste. Heat thoroughly, but don't let it boil.
- Divide the goat's cheese among the serving bowls, sprinkle with the chives, then ladle the soup over and serve.

Broad Bean & Smoked Chicken

Cook this, and your guests will think it's a recipe from a top restaurant. In reality, it's something much simpler: great ingredients seasoned with a twist of imagination.

The freshness of the broad bean and the smokiness of the chicken make for a superb combination. There's also plenty of contrast in textures between the smooth base and the bite of the beans and chicken.

Serve with a flourish of self-confidence; you can't go wrong with this soup.

Serves 4

Cooking time: 45 minutes

500 g (1 lb 2 oz) broad beans

200 g (7 oz) cooked, smoked (or roast) chicken breast

25 g (1 oz) butter

1 medium onion, finely chopped

2 small celery sticks, sliced

1 clove garlic, crushed

1 tablespoon fresh thyme, chopped

750 ml (26 fl. oz) chicken stock

Salt and freshly ground black pepper

- Take 100 g/3$\frac{1}{2}$ oz of the broad beans, blanch in boiling water for 3 minutes, refresh in cold water, then remove the shells. Reserve to decorate the soup.
- Finely slice one quarter of the smoked chicken and set aside for later; roughly chop the remaining.
- Melt the butter in a pan, add the onion, celery and garlic, then cook gently for 5 minutes, without colouring.
- Add the broad beans (and their shells), the roughly chopped chicken, thyme and stock. Bring to the boil, cover and simmer for 15 minutes.
- Blend until smooth.
- Return to the pan and season to taste. If the soup is too thick, adjust as required with a little water.
- Add the reserved shelled broad beans and sliced chicken, then heat for 5 minutes and serve.

Carrot, Sweetcorn & Elderflower

This former Soup of the Month supported the Chelsea Flower Show in 2003. It drew on a range of ingredients to celebrate the breadth of produce in a typical British garden.

For simplicity, we've used elderflower cordial rather than fresh heads of elderflowers. You could, of course, try it earlier in the year (adapting as necessary), when the countryside is awash with elderflowers. Either way, you obtain a beautifully sweet, summery and fragrant soup filled with sweetcorn kernels.

Serves 4

Cooking time: 50 minutes

2 tablespoons olive oil

1 medium onion, finely diced

2 medium carrots, diced

2 celery sticks, finely sliced

700 ml (1¼ pints) vegetable stock

1 tablespoon elderflower cordial

400 g (13 oz) sweetcorn

Salt and freshly ground black pepper

- Heat the olive oil in a pan, add the onion, carrots and celery, then cook for 10 minutes.
- Add the vegetable stock and bring to the boil. Add the elderflower cordial, then cover and cook for 15 minutes until the vegetables are tender.
- Blend until smooth.
- Return to the pan, add the sweetcorn, season to taste, then cook for a further 10 minutes and serve.

Courgette & Tarragon

When courgettes ripen, they come with an unstoppable rush that forces cooks to search for new uses. This is the recipe that Ann Parrott (mum of our marketing director, Nigel) came up with. Her soup freezes well, which means she can cook her courgette glut as it ripens, then store in the freezer for the winter.

When she first made it, Ann had fresh tarragon in the garden. Sadly, it never prospered, so she resorted to dried tarragon without any noticeable loss of flavour.

Serve with a swirl of cream and a sigh of relief that you caught your courgette harvest before it overwhelmed you.

Serves 4

Cooking time: 40 minutes

25 g (1 oz) butter

4 medium courgettes, chunked

1½ tablespoons tarragon, dried chopped

300 ml (10½ fl. oz) vegetable stock

300 ml (10½ fl. oz) milk

Salt and freshly ground pepper

- Melt the butter in a pan, add the courgettes, then cook on a medium heat for 5 minutes.
- Add the tarragon and cook gently for a further 5 minutes.
- Add the stock, which should almost cover the courgettes, then bring to the boil. Cover and simmer for 15 minutes until the courgettes are tender, then add the milk.
- Blend until smooth.
- Return to the pan and season to taste. Reheat gently for 3 minutes and serve.

Watercress, Pear & Brie

This soup has special occasion written all over it. The combination of green leaves, fresh fruit and ripe cheese sounds inviting; the smooth texture and sophisticated tastes are irresistible.

Watercress is a delicate plant with a sharp, peppery flavour. It doesn't need much cooking before it blends to an appealing green. The pepperyness goes well with the acidity of pear and the tang of brie. All you need is a dollop of double cream and you can serve your guests a bowlful of midsummer luxury.

Serves 4

Cooking Time: 40 minutes

- 10 g (½ oz) butter
- 1 small onion diced
- 1 medium potato, diced
- 2 pears, cored and diced
- 490 ml (17½ fl. oz) vegetable stock
- 120 g (4½ oz) watercress
- 65 g (2½ oz) Somerset brie, chopped into chunks
- Salt and freshly ground black pepper
- 1 tablespoon double cream

- Melt the butter in a pan, add the onion and potato and cook for 10 minutes without colouring.
- Add the pears and vegetable stock and cook for 25 minutes until the onion and the potato are soft.
- Add the watercress and cook for a further 3 minutes until it wilts. Add the brie, then cook for 1 minute.
- Blend until smooth, return to the pan, then season to taste.
- Add the double cream, heat gently for 2 minutes and serve.

Roasted Fennel & Somerset Cider

Caroline Bland discovered the delights of Somerset cider when she moved south-west to join our design agency. Soon afterwards, she began experimenting with cider in her dinner-party dishes.

This inventive starter was a success on its first outing. To get the depth of flavour, Caroline roasts fennel and red onions in olive oil, lemon thyme and coriander till lightly caramelized, then roasts again in cider till the sauce turns syrupy. The hard work – the blending and sieving till smooth – comes at the end, followed by the wave of applause that she brushes aside with characteristic modesty.

Serves 4

Cooking time: 1 hour 15 minutes

700 g (1 lb 8 oz) fennel bulbs

2 medium red onions

2 tablespoons olive oil

1 tablespoon coriander seeds

2–3 tablespoons lemon thyme, chopped

300 ml (10½ fl. oz) dry Somerset cider

750 ml (26 fl. oz) chicken stock

150 ml (5 fl. oz) double cream

Salt and freshly ground black pepper

- Preheat the oven to 200°C/gas mark 6.
- Cut the fennel bulbs and red onions into 6 wedges, so that they are of similar sizes.
- Place in a roasting tin, drizzle with the olive oil, sprinkle the coriander seeds and lemon thyme over and toss to ensure all vegetables are covered. Roast for 30 minutes, stirring occasionally, until vegetables are softened with some caramelized edges.
- Pour the cider over the vegetables and roast for a further 15 minutes. The cider should have reduced to a syrupy layer in the roasting tin – don't allow it to dry out.
- Remove from the oven, then blend until smooth, adding the chicken stock as you blend. This will need to be done in batches.
- Once each batch is blended, sieve the soup, pushing it through with the back of a ladle. This takes a little time but is well worth it.
- Return the sieved soup to the pan and add the cream. Season to taste, then reheat for 3 minutes and serve.

Bouillabaisse

There is no fixed recipe for bouillabaisse, the great Provençal fish stew. The best guess is that it began as a dish for fishermen to use up the unsaleable remnants of their catch. So feel free to use your own selection of fish and seafood. The important thing is that it should feel full and chunky – the sort of soup that would satisfy a boatload of tired and hungry fishermen. Or a carload of tired and hungry holidaymakers.

Serves 4

Cooking time: 35 minutes

- 3 tablespoons olive oil
- 3 cloves garlic, crushed
- ½ red onion, chopped
- ½ fennel bulb, finely sliced
- ½ leek, chopped
- 800 ml (28 fl. oz) fish stock
- 400 g (13 oz) chopped tomatoes
- 400 ml (14½ fl. oz) tomato passata
- Pinch of saffron strands, soaked in 2 tablespoons hot water
- ½ red chilli, finely diced
- 3 sprigs thyme
- 1 bay leaf
- ½ orange, zest of
- 3 tablespoons fresh parsley, chopped
- 400 g (13 oz) turbot, filleted, large chunks
- 350 g (12 oz) large raw prawns, tail on
- 2 cooked crabs, meat only

- Heat the olive oil in a pan, add the garlic, red onion, fennel and leek, then cook over a moderate heat, stirring frequently for 5–10 minutes until softened.
- Add the stock, chopped tomatoes, passata, saffron, chilli, thyme, bay leaf, orange zest and 2 tablespoons of the chopped parsley. Bring to the boil and simmer for 15 minutes.
- Add the turbot and cook for 5 minutes. Add the prawns and crab meat, then cook for a further 3–5 minutes until all the fish is cooked.
- Season to taste, sprinkle with the remaining chopped parsley and serve.

Summer Salad

This is the sort of easy, refreshing recipe you want to take on holiday with you. The very appearance of Summer Salad, with its cool green base and bright cherry tomato halves, puts you in mind of shady verandas and lazy afternoons.

Summer Salad is the work of Sarah Lake, the sister of our own inventive chef, Jessica Money. Sarah wanted to create a soup to match the idyllic summers of our imaginations. It had to be almost effortless (there's no cooking in this chilled soup), or it would break the mood of the day. As Sarah puts it, all you need is a deckchair and a blender.

Serves 4

Cooking Time: 15 minutes

2 avocados, skin and stone removed

270 g (10 oz) roundhead lettuce, roughly chopped

1 teaspoon coriander, chopped

2 tablespoons lime juice

410 ml (¾ pint) apple juice, fresh

1 teaspoon parsley, chopped

100 g (3½ oz) cherry tomatoes, two-thirds cut in half

2 spring onions, finely sliced

Salt & freshly ground black pepper

- Place the avocado, lettuce, coriander, lime juice, apple juice, half the parsley and a third of the cherry tomatoes into a blender.
- Blend until smooth.
- Place the blended soup into a bowl, add the remaining chopped parsley, spring onions and cherry tomatoes.
- Season to taste, then stir well and serve.

Summer Pistou

A pistou is a French vegetable soup with Italian origins. The defining ingredient is pesto – the piquant paste of basil, garlic, pine nuts and Parmesan – the French version of which is also known as pistou.

This summer version comes from our engineer, Neil Edwards, who makes his pistou with straightforward simplicity and a pile of chopped seasonal vegetables. It's a fuss-free summer lunch or evening meal that you can serve hot or cold, depending on your mood or the weather.

Serves 4

Cooking time: 30 minutes

1 tablespoon olive oil
1 small onion, chopped
1 clove garlic, finely chopped
300 ml (10 ½ fl. oz) vegetable stock
150 g (5 oz) new potatoes, diced
200 g (7 oz) baby carrots, batons
100 g (3 ½ oz) baby courgettes, batons
2 tomatoes, skinned and chopped
100 g (3 ½ oz) fresh peas, shelled
Salt and freshly ground black pepper
1 tablespoon green pesto

- Heat the olive oil in a pan, add the onion and garlic, then cook gently for 5 minutes until soft, without colouring.
- Add the stock, bring to boil, then add the new potatoes, cover and simmer for 10 minutes.
- Add the carrots, courgettes and tomatoes, then cook for a further 8 minutes, add a little water if required.
- Add the peas and simmer for a further 5 minutes.
- Season to taste, then add the green pesto and serve.

Grouse, Shallot & Thyme

Any creature that lives almost exclusively on purple heather has to taste good. For the cook, that's the appeal of grouse, a game bird with dark meat and a fabulous flavour. The Glorious Twelfth (of August) marks the start of the grouse season and the first day that we can cook our favourite game soup. It's a great dish to come home to after a big day out, walking or cycling with the family in the late-summer sunshine.

Serves 4

Cooking time: 1 hour 45 minutes

1 x 400 g (13 oz) grouse
6 rashers streaky bacon
2 tablespoons olive oil
200 g (7 oz) carrots, diced
2 sticks celery, diced
200 g (7 oz) swede, diced
150 g (5 oz) shallots
250 ml (9 fl. oz) full-bodied red wine
600 ml (21 fl. oz) chicken stock
Salt and freshly ground black pepper
Few sprigs thyme
1 tablespoon rosemary, chopped
1 bay leaf
1 tablespoon parsley, chopped

- Preheat the oven to 150°C/gas mark 2.
- Remove any giblets or down feathers from the grouse. Season and layer the streaky bacon across the breast, secure with string.
- Heat the oil in an ovenproof pan with a tight-fitting lid, add the grouse and brown the skin on all sides; remove from the pan and leave to one side.
- Add the vegetables to the pan, cook for 5 minutes, then add the wine and cook for a further 2 minutes.
- Return the grouse to the pan, add the stock, seasoning and herbs (except the parsley), then slowly bring to the boil.
- Cover the pan and place it in the oven for 1^1/2 hours, stirring occasionally.
- Remove the pan from the oven, take the grouse out and set to one side, allowing to cool slightly.
- Once cooled, skin and strip the meat from the bones.
- Return the shredded meat to the pan, season to taste, then reheat gently for 5 minutes. Stir in the parsley and serve.

Runner Bean & Braised Ham Broth

After an active family day out, you want something quick and nutritious that doesn't take much work. This chunky broth is the answer. It uses up leftover boiled ham and the stock from the boiling of the ham.

If you prepared the vegetables in advance, you can have this soup ready in a quarter of an hour. It may even be on the table before the rest of the family have had time to sort themselves out – bikes locked, helmets stowed, shoes off, hands washed, arguments settled, tummies rumbling.

Serves 4

Cooking time: 15 minutes

850 ml (1½ pints) ham stock

250 g (9 oz) runner beans, sliced

100 g (3½ oz) baby carrots, cut into batons

1 leek, finely sliced

100 g (3½ oz) ham, shredded

1 tablespoon fresh chives, chopped

1 tablespoon fresh parsley, chopped

Salt and freshly ground black pepper

- Place the stock in a pan and bring to the boil.
- Add all the vegetables and ham, then cover and cook rapidly for 5–7 minutes until the vegetables are crisp but tender.
- Add the chopped herbs, season to taste and serve.

Index

Apple

Apple, Vine Tomato & Smoked Bacon, 79

Parsnip, Apple & Chestnut, 53

Roast Pumpkin & Bramley Apple, 29

Simple Parsnip & Apple, 37

Venison, Apple & Blackberry, 35

Apple, Vine Tomato & Smoked Bacon, 79

Apricot

Spicy Chicken, Pea & Apricot, 25

Sweet Potato and Spring fruits, 96

Artichoke

Crab & Artichoke, 109

Cream of, 27

Love & Hearts (Artichoke Hearts & Pancetta), 70

Asparagus

Asparagus, Cucumber & Pea, 99

Asparagus, Leek & New Potato Chowder, 94

Asparagus, Cucumber & Pea, 99

Asparagus, Leek & New Potato Chowder, 94

Avocado

Summer Salad, 119

Baby Vegetable & Minted Lamb Broth, 101

Bacon

Apple, Vine Tomato & Smoked Bacon, 79

Bacon, Broccoli & Celeriac, 34

Broad Bean & Bacon, 90

Savoy Cabbage & Bacon, 87

Bacon, Broccoli & Celeriac, 34

Bangers & Beans, 44

Bean

Baby Vegetable & Minted Lamb Broth, 101

Bangers & Beans, 44

Broad Bean & Bacon, 90

Broad Bean & Garlic, 108

Broad Bean & Smoked Chicken, 113

Broad Bean, Feta Cheese & Smoked Salmon, 102

Runner Bean & Braised Ham Broth, 122

Beautiful Broccoli, 107

Beef

Beef, Ale & Wild Mushroom, 39

Russian Beef Borsch, 68

Beef Stock, 13

Beef, Ale & Wild Mushroom, 39

Beetroot

Beetroot & Rhubarb, 80

Beetroot, Raspberry & Sparkling Wine, 26

Russian Beef Borsch, 68

Beetroot & Rhubarb, 80

Beetroot, Raspberry & Sparkling Wine, 26

Berry

Strawberry, Cream & Champagne, 111

Summer Berry, 106

Summer Fruits with Mango Custard, 110

Blackberry

Venison, Apple & Blackberry, 35

Bouillabaisse, 118

Broad Bean & Bacon, 90

Broad Bean & Garlic, 108

Broad Bean & Smoked Chicken, 113

Broad Bean, Feta Cheese & Smoked Salmon, 102

Broccoli

Bacon, Broccoli & Celeriac, 34

Beautiful Broccoli, 107

Purple Sprouting Broccoli & Leek, 60

Brussel Sprout

Brussel Sprout & Gammon, 50

Leftover Soup, 52

Brussel Sprout & Gammon, 50

Butternut Squash

Butternut Squash, Cromer Crab & Chilli, 82

Butternut Squash, Orange & Ginger, 64

Simple Butternut Squash, 74

Sweet Potato, Butternut Squash & Smoked Chilli, 30

Butternut Squash, Cromer Crab & Chilli, 82

Butternut Squash, Orange & Ginger, 64

Caramelized Root Vegetable, 38

Carrot
  Baby Vegetable & Minted Lamb Broth, 101
  Caramelized Root Vegetable, 38
  Carrot & Ginger, 51
  Carrot, Mango & Cumin, 103
  Carrot, Sweetcorn & Elderflower, 114
  Honey Glazed Chantenay Carrot, 43
  New Year Root Vegetable, 55
  Pumpkin & Scary Carrot, 36
Carrot & Ginger, 51
Carrot, Mango & Cumin, 103
Carrot, Sweetcorn & Elderflower, 114
Cauliflower
  Cauliflower & Almond, 85
  Cauliflower & Vintage Cheddar, 28
  Cauliflower, Mustard & Gorgonzola Cheese, 56
Cauliflower & Almond, 85
Cauliflower & Vintage Cheddar, 28
Cauliflower, Mustard & Gorgonzola Cheese, 56
Celeriac
  Bacon, Broccoli & Celeriac, 34
  Cream of Celeriac & Truffle, 49
Champagne & Camembert, 59
Chicken
  Broad Bean & Smoked Chicken, 113
  Cock-A-Leekie, 40
  Heart-Warming Chicken Broth, 66
  Spicy Chicken, Pea & Apricot, 25
Chicken Stock, 14
Chocolate
  Chocolate & Rhubarb Swirl, 88
Chocolate & Rhubarb Swirl, 88
Christmas Dinner Soup, 54
Cock-A-Leekie, 40
Courgette
  Courgette & Tarragon, 115
  Mediterranean Vegetable & Tomato, 24
  Summer Pistou, 120
Courgette & Tarragon, 115

Crab
  Butternut Squash, Cromer Crab & Chilli, 82
  Crab & Artichoke, 109
Crab & Artichoke, 109
Cream of Artichoke, 27
Cream of Celeriac & Truffle, 49
Creamy Baked Garlic & Onion, 67
Cucumber
  Asparagus, Cucumber & Pea, 99
Cullen Skink, 41
Duck
  Duck & Pomegranate, 48
Duck & Pomegranate, 48
Fennel
  Roasted Fennel & Somerset Cider, 117
  Tomato, Fennel & Feta, 23
Fish
  Bouillabaisse, 118
  Cullen Skink, 41
  Oyster, Tomato & Saffron, 63
  Smoked Mackerel & Horseradish, 100
  Trout & Watercress, 22
  Wild Salmon Chowder, 77
Fish Stock, 17
Game
  Grouse, Shallot & Thyme, 121
  Pheasant & Roasted Shallot, 31
  Venison, Apple & Blackberry, 35
  Venison Sausage Cassoulet, 75
  Wood Pigeon & Morel Mushroom, 81
Garlic
  Creamy Baked Garlic & Onion, 67
  Mussel, White Wine & Garlic, 21
  Turnip, Honey & Roasted Garlic, 78
  Broad Bean & Garlic, 108
Goat's Cheese
  Potato, Sorrel & Goat's Cheese, 112
Grouse, Shallot & Thyme, 121
Haddock
  Cullen Skink, 41

Haggis, Neeps & Tatties, 61
Ham
    Runner Bean & Braised Ham Broth, 122
Heart-Warming Chicken Broth, 66
Honey Glazed Chantenay Carrot, 43
Hungarian Lamb, 92
Jerusalem Artichoke
    Jerusalem Artichoke & Porcini Mushroom, 47
Jerusalem Artichoke & Porcini Mushroom, 47
Lamb
    Baby Vegetable & Minted Lamb Broth, 101
    Hungarian Lamb, 92
Lamb Stock, 16
Leek
    Asparagus, Leek & New Potato Chowder, 94
    Caramelized Root Vegetable, 38
    Cock-A-Leekie, 40
    New Year Root Vegetable, 55
    Purple Sprouting Broccoli & Leek, 60
Leftover Soup, 52
Lentil
    Spicy Turnip & Lentil Dhal, 86
Lettuce
    Pea, Herb & Lettuce, 93
    Radish, Spring Onion & Lettuce, 95
    Summer Salad, 119
Lobster Bisque, 89
Love & Hearts (Artichoke Hearts & Pancetta), 70
Mackerel
    Smoked Mackerel & Horseradish, 100
Mango
    Carrot, Mango & Cumin, 103
    Summer Fruits with Mango Custard, 110
Maple Roast Parsnip, 33
Mediterranean Vegetable & Tomato, 24
Mushroom
    Beef, Ale & Wild Mushroom, 39
    Jerusalem Artichoke & Porcini Mushroom, 47
    Mushroom, Stilton & White Wine, 58
    Wood Pigeon & Morel Mushroom, 81
Mushroom, Stilton & White Wine, 58

Mussel
    Mussel, White Wine & Garlic, 21
    Spicy Mussels, 57
Mussel, White Wine & Garlic, 21
New Year Root Vegetable, 55
Onion
    Creamy Baked Garlic & Onion,67
    White Onion, 84
Oyster
    Oyster, Tomato & Saffron, 63
Oyster, Tomato & Saffron, 63
Pak Choi & Chilli, 62
Parsnip
    Caramelized Root Vegetable, 38
    Maple Roast Parsnip, 33
    New Year Root Vegetable, 55
    Parsnip, Apple & Chestnut, 53
    Roasted Parsnip, Lemon & Vanilla, 73
    Simple Parsnip & Apple, 37
Parsnip, Apple & Chestnut, 53
Pea
    Asparagus, Cucumber & Pea, 99
    Baby Vegetable & Minted Lamb Broth, 101
    Pea, Herb & Lettuce, 93
    Petits Pois and Watercress, 91
    Spicy Chicken, Pea & Apricot, 25
    Summer Pistou, 120
Pea, Herb & Lettuce, 93
Pear
    Pear, Roquefort & Spinach, 42
    Watercress, Pear & Brie, 116
Pear, Roquefort & Spinach, 42
Pepper
    Sweet Potato & Red Pepper Chowder, 32
Petits Pois and Watercress, 91
Pheasant
    Pheasant & Roasted Shallot, 31
Pheasant & Roasted Shallot, 31
Pomegranate
    Duck & Pomegranate, 48
Potato, Sorrel & Goat's Cheese, 112

Potatoes, New
    Asparagus, Leek & New Potato Chowder, 94
    Summer Pistou, 120
    Watercress & New Potato, 105
    Wild Salmon Chowder, 77
Pumpkin
    Pumpkin & Scary Carrot, 36
    Roast Pumpkin & Bramley Apple, 29
Pumpkin & Scary Carrot, 36
Purple Sprouting Broccoli & Leek, 60
Radish
    Radish, Spring Onion & Lettuce, 95
Radish, Spring Onion & Lettuce, 95
Raspberry
    Beetroot, Raspberry & Sparkling Wine, 26
Rhubarb
    Beetroot & Rhubarb, 80
    Chocolate & Rhubarb Swirl, 88
    Sweet Potato and Spring Fruits, 96
Roast Pumpkin & Bramley Apple, 29
Roasted Fennel & Somerset Cider, 117
Roasted Parsnip, Lemon & Vanilla, 73
Runner Bean & Braised Ham Broth, 122
Russian Beef Borsch, 68
Salmon
    Broad Bean, Feta Cheese & Smoked
      Salmon, 102
    Wild Salmon Chowder, 77
Savoy Cabbage
    Savoy Cabbage & Bacon, 87
Savoy Cabbage & Bacon, 87
Shallot
    Grouse, Shallot & Thyme, 121
    Pheasant & Roasted Shallot, 31
Simple Butternut Squash, 74
Simple Parsnip & Apple, 37
Simply Swede, 69
Smoked Mackerel & Horseradish, 100
Sorrel
    Potato, Sorrel & Goat's Cheese, 112
    Summer Sorrel, Swiss Chard & Lemon
      Thyme, 104
Spicy Chicken, Pea & Apricot, 25

Spicy Mussels, 57
Spicy Turnip & Lentil Dhal, 86
Spinach
    Pear, Roquefort & Spinach, 42
    Spinach, Parsley & Honey, 76
    Spinach, Stilton & White Wine, 65
Spinach, Parsley & Honey, 76
Spinach, Stilton & White Wine, 65
Spring Greens, 83
Spring Onion
    Radish, Spring Onion & Lettuce, 95
Stocks
    Beef, 13
    Chicken, 14
    Fish, 17
    Lamb, 16
    Vegetable, 15
Strawberry, Cream & Champagne, 111
Summer Berry, 106
Summer Fruits with Mango Custard, 110
Summer Pistou, 120
Summer Salad, 119
**Summer Sorrel, Swiss Chard & Lemon
    Thyme, 104**
Swede
    Caramelized Root Vegetable, 38
    Haggis, Neeps & Tatties, 61
    Simply Swede, 69
Sweet Potato
    New Year Root Vegetable, 55
    Sweet Potato & Red Pepper Chowder, 32
    Sweet Potato and Spring Fruits, 96
    Sweet Potato, Butternut Squash & Smoked
      Chilli, 30
Sweet Potato & Red Pepper Chowder, 32
Sweet Potato and Spring Fruits, 96
Sweet Potato, Butternut Squash & Smoked Chilli, 30
Sweetcorn
    Carrot, Sweetcorn & Elderflower, 114
    Sweet Potato & Red Pepper Chowder, 32
Swiss Chard
    Summer Sorrel, Swiss Chard & Lemon
      Thyme, 104

Tarragon
    Courgette & Tarragon, 115
Tomato
    Apple, Vine Tomato & Smoked Bacon, 79
    Mediterranean Vegetable & Tomato, 24
    Oyster, Tomato & Saffron, 63
    Tomato, Fennel & Feta, 23
Tomato, Fennel & Feta, 23
Trout
    Trout & Watercress, 22
Trout & Watercress, 22
Turnip
    Caramelized Root Vegetable, 38
    Spicy Turnip & Lentil Dhal, 86
    Turnip, Honey & Roasted Garlic, 78
Turnip, Honey & Roasted Garlic, 78

Vegetable Stock, 15
Venison
    Venison, Apple & Blackberry, 35
    Venison Sausage Cassoulet, 75
Venison, Apple & Blackberry, 35
Venison Sausage Cassoulet, 75
Watercress
    Petits Pois and Watercress, 91
    Trout & Watercress, 22
    Watercress & New Potato, 105
    Watercress, Pear & Brie, 116
Watercress & New Potato, 105
Watercress, Pear & Brie, 116
White Onion, 84
Wild Salmon Chowder, 77
Wood Pigeon & Morel Mushroom, 81